Playing Smart

Playful Thinking

Jesper Juul, Geoffrey Long, and William Uricchio, editors

...lligence

Julian Togelius

The MIT Press
Cambridge, Massachusetts
London, England

This book was set in ITC Stone Serif Std by Toppan Best-set Premedia Limited. Printed and bound in the United States of America.

Library of Congress Cataloging-in-Publication Data

Names: Togelius, Julian, author.
Title: Playing smart : on games, intelligence and Artificial Intelligence / Julian Togelius.
Description: Cambridge, MA : MIT Press, [2018] | Series: Playful thinking | Includes bibliographical references and index.
Identifiers: LCCN 2018010191 | ISBN 9780262039031 (hardcover : alk. paper)
Subjects: LCSH: Video games--Psychological aspects. | Video games--Design. | Intellect. | Thought and thinking. | Artificial intelligence.
Classification: LCC GV1469.34.P79 T64 2018 | DDC 794.8--dc23 LC record available at https://lccn.loc.gov/2018010191

10   9   8   7   6   5   4   3   2   1

Contents

On Thinking Playfully

Many people (we series editors included) find video games exhilarating, but it can be just as interesting to ponder why that is so. What do video games do? What can they be used for? How do they work? How do they relate to the rest of the world? Why is play both so important and so powerful?

Playful Thinking is a series of short, readable, and argumentative books that share some playfulness and excitement with the games that they are about. Each book in the series is small enough to fit in a backpack or coat pocket, and combines depth with readability for any reader interested in playing more thoughtfully or thinking more playfully. This includes, but is by no means limited to, academics, game makers, and curious players.

So we are casting our net wide. Each book in our series provides a blend of new insights and interesting arguments with overviews of knowledge from game studies and other areas. You will see this reflected not just in the range of titles in our series, but in the range of authors creating them. Our basic assumption is simple: video games are such a flourishing medium that any new perspective on them is likely to show us something unseen or forgotten, including those from such unconventional voices as artists, philosophers, or specialists in other industries or fields of study. These books are bridge builders, cross-pollinating both areas with new knowledge and new ways of thinking.

At its heart, this is what Playful Thinking is all about: new ways of thinking about games and new ways of using games to think about the rest of the world.

Jesper Juul
Geoffrey Long
William Uricchio

Prologue: AI&I

I was eleven when my cats had to be given away because my mother had discovered she was allergic to them. Of course, I was very sad about the departure of my cats, but not so much that I wouldn't accept a Commodore 64 as a bribe to not protest too loudly. The Commodore 64 was already an obsolete computer in 1990; now, operational Commodore 64s are mostly owned by museums and hipsters.

I quickly became very engrossed in my Commodore 64, more than I had been in my cats, because the computer was more interactive and understandable. Or rather, there was the hint of a possibility to understand it. I played the various games that I had received with the computer on about a dozen cassette tapes—loading a game could take several minutes and frequently failed, testing the very limited patience of an eleven-year-old—and marveled at the depth of possibilities contained within those games. Although I had not yet learned how to program, I knew that the computer obeyed strict rules all the way and that there was really no magic to it, and I loved that. This also helped me see the limitations of these games. It was very easy to win some games by noticing that certain actions always evoked certain responses and certain things always happened in the same order. The fierce and enormous ant I battled at the end of the first level in *Giana Sisters* really had an extremely simple pattern of actions, limited by the hardware of the time. But that did not lessen my determination to get past it.

You could argue that the rich and complex world of these games existed as much in my imagination as in actual computer memory. I knew that the ant boss in *Giana Sisters* moved just two steps forward and one step backward regardless of what I did, or that the enemy spaceships in *Defender* simply moved in a straight line toward my position wherever I was on the screen. But I wanted there to be so much more. I wanted there to be secret, endless worlds to explore within these games, characters with lives of their own, a never-emptying treasure trove of secrets to discover. Above all, I wanted there to be things happening that I could not predict, but which still made sense for whoever inside the game made them happen.

In comparison, my cats were mostly unpredictable and gave every sign of living a life of their own that I knew very little about. But sometimes they were very predictable. Pull a string, and the cat would jump at it; open a can of cat food, and the cat would come running. After spending time among the rule-based inhabitants of computer games, I started wondering whether the cats' behaviors could be explained the same way. Were their minds just sets of rules specifying computations? And if so, was the same thing true for humans?

Because I wanted to create games, I taught myself programming. I had bought a more capable computer with the proceeds from a summer job when I was thirteen and found a compiler for the now-antiquated programming language Turbo Pascal on that computer's hard drive. I started by simply modifying other people's code to see what happened until I knew enough to write my own games. I rapidly discovered that making good games was hard. Designing games was hard, and creating in-game agents that behaved in an even remotely intelligent manner was very hard.

After finishing high school I did not want to do anything mathematical (I was terrible at math and hated it).[1] I wanted to understand the mind, so I started studying philosophy and psychology at Lund University. I gradually realized, however, that to really understand the mind, I needed to build one, so I drifted into computer science and studied artificial intelligence. For my PhD, I was, in a way, back to animals. I was interested in applying the kind of mechanisms we see in "simple" animals (the ones that literally don't have that many brain cells) to controlling robots and also in using simulations of natural evolution to learn these mechanisms. The problem was that the experiments I wanted to do would require thousands or even tens of thousands of repetitions, which would take a lot of time. Also, real robots frequently break down and require service, so these experiments would need me to be on standby as a robot mechanic, something I was not interested in. Physical machines are boring and annoying; it's the ideas behind them that are exciting.

Then it struck me: Why don't I simply use games instead of robots? Games are cheaper and simpler to experiment with than robots, and the experiments can be run much faster. And there are so many challenges in playing games—challenges that must be worth caring about because humans care a lot about them. So while my friends worked with mobile robots that clumsily made their way around the lab and frequently needed their tires adjusted and batteries changed, I worked with racing games, *StarCraft*, and *Super Mario Bros*. I had a lot of fun. In the process, it became clear to me that not only could games be used to test and develop artificial intelligence (AI), but that AI could be used to make games better—AI for games as well as games for AI. For example, could we use AI methods to automatically design new game levels? Noting that there were ample possibilities for using modern AI methods to improve games, I started thinking about game design and how games could be designed with these modern methods, as well as human thinking in mind.

I had come full circle. I was once again thinking about intelligence and artificial intelligence through the lens of games, and about games through the lenses of intelligence and artificial intelligence, just like when I was eleven. It is fair to say that I have spent most of my life thinking about these interrelated topics in one way or another, and I'd like to think that I've learned a thing or two. I hope that I can intelligibly convey some of my enthusiasm as well as some of the substance of the research field I'm part of in this book.

What Is This Book?

This is a book about games, intelligence, and artificial intelligence. In particular, it is a book about how these three things relate to each other. I explain how games help us understand what intelligence is and what artificial intelligence is, and how artificial intelligence helps us understand games. I also explain how artificial intelligence can help us make better games and how games can help us invent better artificial intelligence. My whole career has been based on my conviction that games, intelligence, and artificial intelligence are deeply and multiply intertwined. I wrote this book to help you see these topics in the light of each other.

This is a popular science book in the sense that it does not require you to be trained in, or even familiar with, any particular field of inquiry to read it. You don't need to know anything about artificial intelligence, and although I explain several important algorithms throughout the book, it is entirely free of mathematical notation—you can follow the argument even if you only skim the descriptions of algorithms. Some familiarity with basic programming concepts is useful but not necessary. You don't need to know anything about game studies, game design, or psychology, either. The only real prerequisite is that you care about games and occasionally play games. It doesn't really matter which games.

In other words, I wrote this book for both members of the general public who are curious about games and AI and people who work with games in some way (perhaps by making them, studying them, or writing about them) but don't know much about AI. If you are already knowledgeable about AI, I hope you will still find the book interesting, though you may want to skim some parts.

This book is also a scholarly argument, or rather several arguments. It is an argument that games have always been important—perhaps even a driving force—in artificial intelligence research, and that the role of games in AI research is about to become even more important, with the ongoing switch from board games to video games as the AI benchmarks of choice and the advent of general video game playing, which allows us to benchmark the general thinking skills of programs. Conversely, artificial intelligence has always been important in games, even though many game developers have been unaware of AI research. But we are likely to see AI becoming much more important to future games—in particular, video games—both because of advances in AI methods and because of new ideas on which roles AI can be used in in games. Although in the past it was commonly assumed that the AI in a game was all about how the computer-controlled characters you met in a game behaved, we now see AI being used to understand players, adapt games by changing the levels, and even help us create new games.

I make three primary claims in this book:

- Games are the future of AI. Games provide the best benchmarks for AI because of the way they are designed to challenge many different human cognitive abilities, as well as for their technical convenience and the availability of human data. We have only begun to scratch the surface of game-based AI benchmarks.

- AI is the future of games. We now have much more capable AI methods than just a few years ago, and we are rapidly learning how to best apply them to games. The potential roles of AI in games go far beyond providing skillful opponents. We need to adapt our ways of thinking about game design to fully harness the power of advanced AI algorithms and enable a new generation of AI-augmented games.

- Games and AI for games help us understand intelligence. By studying how humans play and design games, we can understand how they think, and we can attempt to replicate this thinking by creating game-playing and game-designing AI agents. Game design is a cognitive science; it studies thinking—human thinking and machine thinking.

The book is fairly liberally sprinkled with footnotes.[1] I've tried to relegate everything that would break the flow of the text into the footnotes. In particular, I put almost all my citations in footnotes. Feel free to entirely disregard these if you want to.

I have also written this book in a relatively informal and relaxed, sometimes even playful, tone. This is both in order to make it more readable outside the ivory tower of academia and because this is the way I naturally write. I think that most academic writing is needlessly formal and rather boring. I promise you that nothing I say is less true because I use the active tense and even the first-person singular pronoun.

This is where I give you an overview of the book. Chapter 1 starts from the beginning, with the origin of computers and some ancient games and fundamental algorithms. The very first computer scientists tried to develop programs that could play classic board games such as Chess, as these were thought to embody the core of intelligence. Eventually we succeeded in constructing software that beat us at all board games. But does this mean that this software is intelligent? Chapter 2 asks whether you need to be intelligent to play games (or to play games well). It seems that not only do games do a good job of exercising your brain in a number of different ways, they also teach you to play them; in fact, well-designed games are finely tuned to the abilities of humans. But if they require intelligence from you, how can an algorithm play them without being intelligent? Chapter 3 digs into the question of whether a game-playing program can be (or have) artificial intelligence, and if not, what AI actually is. There are several ideas about what intelligence and artificial intelligence are, but none of these ideas is without its own problems. While we may still not know just what intelligence or AI is, we now know a lot more about what it is not.

Next, in chapter 4, we look at what kind of AI you actually would find in a modern video game. I describe a couple of important algorithms in the context of a fairly standard shooter game and point out some of the severe limitations of current game AI. But do we even know what AI in a video game would be like if it were not so limited? I try to give some ideas about what it could be like and some ideas about why we do not already have such awesome AI. This certainly has to do with the current state of AI research, but just as much with game design and game development practices. The next three chapters look at some new ways in which AI could be used in games. Chapter 5 describes how nonplayer characters (NPCs)—and other things in a game— could learn by experience, from playing the game, using principles from biology (evolution) and psychology (learning from reinforcements). Chapter 6 describes how games can learn from the humans that play them, and perhaps adapt themselves, and chapter 7 describes how AI can be used in a creative role, to construct or generate parts of games or even complete games. These uses of AI do not necessarily fit well into standard game design and game development practices. Chapter 8 is therefore dedicated to ways of designing games that foreground interesting AI capabilities. For the penultimate chapter, chapter 9, we again turn to the use of games as tests of (artificial) intelligence. Building on the discussion in the previous chapters, I discuss testing and developing AI though general video game playing. Finally, chapter 10 returns to the three claims I advanced above, showing how progress on artificial intelligence for games and progress on games for artificial intelligence are dependent on each other. If you finish this book and still want to know more about games, intelligence, and artificial intelligence, you will be delighted to find a "further reading" section following chapter 10 that suggests books, conference proceedings, and journals that will satisfy your curiosity—or get you started on your own research.

1 In the Beginning of AI, There Were Games

The first working digital computers were developed in the late 1940s or early 1950s, depending on your exact definition of *computer*, and they were immediately used to play games. In fact, in at least one instance, a program for playing a game was written and executed by hand, using pen and paper because a sufficiently powerful computer to run the program had not been built yet. The eager inventor (and player) was none other than Alan Turing, one of the founding fathers of computer science and artificial intelligence. The year was 1948. The game was Chess (figure 1.1). Turing acted as the computer (computing all the moves by hand) when using this algorithm to play against a good friend.[1]

Why Chess? Well, it's a game that's been around for a very long time, the rules are simple to write down in both English and in computer code, and many people play it. For some reason— or some combination of reasons—Chess has traditionally been taken very seriously. Maybe this is because it is seldom, if ever, played for money, which in turn may be because there is no element of chance and no hidden information (no dice or cards and you can see the whole board). Maybe it is because Chess has plenty of depth: there is a lot to learn about playing the game,

Figure 1.1
Chess existed for thousands of years before it became central to artificial intelligence research. (Courtesy of Wikimedia Commons under a Creative Commons 3.0 license.)

so you can keep getting better at the game all your life. The game allows a multitude of different strategies, and master-level players typically have recognizable playing styles.

So it was not far-fetched when, at the very beginning of research into artificial intelligence, Chess was proposed as an important problem to work on. It was inconceivable that anyone could be able to play it at a high level without being truly intelligent, for how could you play this game without successfully planning ahead, judging the true value of board positions, and understanding your opponent's thinking and predicting her moves? The game seemed to be close to pure thought. Or could you think of any other activity that more clearly required intelligence than playing Chess? It seemed natural to assume that if we constructed a program that was a master Chess player, we would have solved the problem of artificial intelligence. So people got to work on this nicely well-defined problem.

While Turing himself was probably the first person to execute a Chess-playing program, many other researchers saw this as an important topic. Chess playing grew into a vibrant subfield of artificial intelligence research, with conferences, journals, and competitions devoted to the study and development of software that could play Chess and similar board games. Several important developments in artificial intelligence took place in the context of board games, such as when the IBM computer scientist Arthur Samuel in 1958 invented the first version of what is now called reinforcement learning in order to make a Checkers-playing program learn from experience.[2]

When the first Chess-playing programs were developed, many thought that a computer program could never rival a master-level human player because these programs were merely code and humans were intelligent. And Chess, mind you, is a sophisticated game that requires intelligence to play.

But during decades of dedicated research, Chess-playing software got stronger and stronger. Whereas these programs initially could barely beat a beginner, they gradually inched their way past intermediate performance, and approached master-level play. This had much to do with the availability of faster processors and larger memory sizes, but it also had a lot to do with the software getting better—essentially refinements of and additions to the same basic algorithm that all of these programs had used from the start.

In 1997 this development finally caught up with the human state-of-the-art, which had been improving slowly, if at all. In a much-publicized match, IBM fielded its special-purpose Deep Blue Chess computer against the reigning world champion, Garry Kasparov. The computer won.[3] This event was the starting point for a vivid debate about the meaning of intelligence and artificial intelligence now that machines had conquered Chess. Most observers concluded that Deep Blue was not really intelligent at all, because it looked and functioned nothing like the human brain. At the heart of Deep Blue is a simple algorithm, though augmented by a myriad bells and whistles. In fact, this algorithm is the very same algorithm that Turing (re)invented in the 1940s. So how does it work?

How a Computer Plays Chess

The approach almost all Chess-playing programs take is to use some variant of the *minimax* algorithm. This is actually a very simple algorithm. It works with the concepts of board states and moves. A board state is the position of all pieces on the board, and a move is a transition from one state to another (for example, moving your pawn two steps forward will transition your board into a state similar to but distinct from the state the board was in before the move). From any board state, it's quite simple to list all moves that a player can take; on average you can take thirty-five or so different moves, and on the first turn, you have twenty moves to choose from. Sometimes you can take only one or two different moves—when this happens, you usually have a problem. Minimax presumes that you can store multiple board states in memory or, in other words, that you can keep lots of copies of the game. (This is not a problem on any modern computer, as a Chess board state can be represented in just a few bytes.)

Minimax also assumes that you have a way of evaluating the value (or utility, or goodness) of a board state. For now, you can think of the value of a board state as how many pieces you've got left on the board, minus how many pieces your opponent has. If the resulting number is positive, you're probably ahead in the game.

Here is how minimax works. Imagine you play from the perspective of the white player, and want to know the best move to take from a particular board state. You start with listing all possible moves you could make from that state. You then simulate taking each move and store all of the resulting board states. If you were very shortsighted, you could stop here; simply estimate the value of each resulting board state (for example, by counting pieces) and choose the move that leads to the board state with the highest value. That would be the *max* part of the minimax algorithm.

That would indeed be shortsighted, however, because a move that brings an immediate benefit (for example, by capturing one of the opponent's pieces) might give the opponent an opening to strike back with one or several captures of her own, thus being disastrous in the slightly less short term. Everyone who has played more than one game of Chess knows this. Therefore, for each of the board states resulting from your possible first moves, you list all possible moves by the opponent and evaluate the resulting board states. The crucial difference to what you did in the first step is that while in the first step you wanted to find the move that was best for you, in the second step, you assume that the opponent will take the move that is most advantageous for her, that is, the worst move for you. If your opponent can capture your piece when it's her turn, she will. That's the *min* part of the minimax algorithm. Putting them together, the best move for you is the one that minimizes the maximum score your opponent can reach in her turn. Practically, for each of your possible moves in your turn, you assign the lowest value of the board that your opponent can reach through any of her moves in the second turn.

You are now looking two turns ahead. However, what of those clever strategies where you let your enemy make a capture on her turn just so you yourself can make a bigger capture on your next turn? Well, you could simply let the minimax algorithm run one step further and assume that the opponent will assume that you do the move that benefits you best. This could go on forever, or until you have reached the end of the game in your simulations. In fact, if you simulate all the way to the end of the game, exploring all moves and all responses to those moves, you will find the provably optimal strategy, one that cannot be improved on. In other words, you will play Chess perfectly.

But you are not going to simulate all the way to the end of the game because you don't have the time to do so. If there are thirty possible moves from one board state (a typical number for midgame Chess), then each turn you simulate will multiply the number of board states you need to investigate by thirty. In other words, you need to evaluate 30^t states, where t is the number of turns you look ahead. For looking five steps ahead, that's about twenty-four million. The number of states you need to investigate quickly approaches the number of atoms in the earth and other such ridiculous numbers. Searching to the end of a Chess game is therefore impossible for any computer we will be able to construct in the foreseeable future. That is why you need a good way of estimating the value of a board state, because you will have to be content with looking only a few turns ahead.

In practice, what a Chess-playing agent does is search to a given depth and then evaluate the board states it reaches even though those are not typically win or loss states. Luckily, in Chess a simple board state estimation such as the piece difference between black and white generally works fairly well, though many more complex methods have been developed.

Minimax is called a *tree-search algorithm*, not because it helps you looking for the most delicious cherries in a cherry tree, but because of what it does can be understood as growing a branching tree as it searches for the best move—a tree that grows upside down. Think of it this way: the root of the tree is the original board state, the one you want to find the best move for. All of the possible moves from that state become branches that grow from the root. At the end of each branch is the board state that move leads to. Of course, from each of these states, a number of moves are possible, and these can in turn be visualized as branches from the end of the previous branch ... and so it continues until you reach those board states where you do not try any more moves but instead estimate the value of the state. Those are called "leaves," in this somewhat imperfect analogy. (Computer scientists are not famous for their analogies.) The number of moves possible at each state is called the "branching factor."

Of course, there have been a number of improvements to this method since Alan Turing himself first suggested it in the 1940s. There are ways of "pruning" the search so that fewer board states are investigated, there are ways of concentrating on the most promising move sequences, and there are much better ways of estimating the value of a board. But the minimax principle remains. It is the core of almost all successful Chess-playing programs.

Advance Directly to Go

Go is a game that occupies a similar place in East Asian culture as Chess does in European culture.[4] It has other things in common with Chess as well, such as having two players, perfect information, no randomness, and that one player uses white pieces and the other black (figure 1.2). In other respects, it is actually simpler. It has only two or three rules, depending on how you count, and one type of piece compared to eight in Chess.

Perhaps somewhat surprisingly, the same methods that work very well for playing Chess fail miserably when it comes to Go. Minimax-based algorithms generally play this game badly. There seem to be two main reasons for this: the branching factor (number of moves) is much higher (on the order of 350 rather than the 35 in Chess), and it is very hard to accurately estimate the value of a board state. The high branching factor means that

Figure 1.2
Go, the simpler but harder (for a computer) Asian cousin of Chess. (Photo by Linh Nguyen under Creative Commons 2.0 license.)

minimax can make only very shallow searches, and the difficulty with estimating the board value means that the "signal" that the minimax algorithm uses is worse. But for a long time, we did not know any better algorithms for playing Go. Therefore, the best Go-playing programs were stuck at beginner level, even as Chess-playing programs reached and surpassed grandmaster level.

So it's natural that people's eyes turned to Go after Chess was conquered. Go seemed so much harder than Chess. Maybe this game could not be conquered with such simplistic techniques? Maybe this game would actually require intelligence to play?

We finally started to see some real progress on Go-playing software in 2007 when the Monte Carlo tree search (MCTS) algorithm was invented.[5] Like minimax, MCTS is a tree search algorithm. Unlike minimax, it has randomness. (That's why it has "Monte Carlo," like the famous Monaco casino, in its name.) Accepting the fact that it will be impossible to explore all possible moves to the same degree, MCTS chooses which moves to explore first randomly; it then proceeds to explore further which of those moves seem most promising initially. Instead of counting pieces to estimate the value of a board (this works very badly in Go), MCTS plays the game randomly until the end many times, and it sees what percentage of these "playouts" it wins. It might seem crazy with so much randomness in the algorithm, but empirically this works very well.

Almost twenty years after Deep Blue's victory over Garry Kasparov, human supremacy in Go was overturned. This time it was the AI research company DeepMind, at the time a division of Google, that provided the software. In a series of matches in 2016, DeepMind's AlphaGo took on Lee Sedol, arguably the world's best Go player, and won 4–1. AlphaGo was built on the

MCTS algorithm, combined with neural networks that had been trained for months on previous matches of numerous Go champions, and by playing against itself (I'll discuss neural networks later in the book).[6]

This was the last important classic board game to yield to the machines.[7] It was also the hardest. There are no longer any classic board games that the best human plays better than the best computer program, at least not classic board games that people care about.

So was AlphaGo intelligent? Most people would say no. Although it functioned differently from Deep Blue and included an element of learning, it was still nothing like the human brain. "Just an algorithm," some would say. And it could only play Go. If could not even play Chess (without re-training its network), nor could it drive a car or write a poem.

This brings up several important questions: Does a thing need to function anything like the human brain in order to be intelligent? And do you need to be intelligent in order to play games well? Let's try to answer the second question first.

2   Do You Need to Be Intelligent to Play Games?

Shall we play a game? You choose: Chess, *Super Mario Bros.*, or *Angry Birds*. I'm giving you a choice because I don't know whether you are familiar with all three of them. I talked about Chess in the previous chapter: the Western's world's arguably most famous board game, played by physically moving pieces such as pawns, kings, and queens on a board with alternating black and white squares. By moving these pieces so that they threaten and capture your opponent's pieces, you can ultimately win over your opponent by surrounding her king. It has changed little since it was invented millennia ago.

Super Mario Bros. is the platform game that accompanied the European/American launch of Nintendo's 8-bit Nintendo Entertainment System (NES) console back in 1985 (figure 2.1). By pressing buttons on a little plastic box, you commandeer the jovial plumber, Mario, as he avoids evil turtles, stomps menacing mushroom men, jumps over gaps, collects coins, and saves the princess who has been kidnapped by a giant lizard. Sequels of the game keep being developed for all of Nintendo's hardware and in addition to hundreds of millions of copies of the *Super Mario Bros.* games that have been sold legitimately, there

Figure 2.1
The genre-defining platform game *Super Mario Bros.* (Nintendo, 1985).

are dozens of unauthorized versions of the game available for any conceivable hardware platform.

Angry Birds is the mobile gaming phenomenon from 2009 by Finnish company Rovio (figure 2.2). You point at and swipe your fingers over your phone's touch screen to fling an assortment of birds at various structures, and your goal is to make the structures collapse on top of evil green pigs that have stolen your eggs. The original game, as well as a myriad of sequels are available for iPhone, iPad, and Android devices and have topped best-seller lists on all those platforms.

Figure 2.2
Angry Birds (Rovio, 2009), the physics puzzler that was on seemingly everyone's iPhone after it debuted.

My guess is that you have played all three of these games, or at least seen someone play them. If not, you have probably played two of them, or at very least one of them. In the extremely unlikely event that you don't know either Chess, *Super Mario Bros.*, or *Angry Birds*, I'm somewhat confused as to who you are and what world you live in. Are you reading this book in the far future? I'm just going to assume you play games of some sort.

Having ascertained that you play games, let me now ask: Why do you play games? To relax, have a good time, lose yourself a bit? Perhaps as a way of socializing with friends? Almost certainly not as some sort of brain exercise. But let's look at what you are really doing:

You plan. In Chess, you are planning for your victory by imagining a sequence of several moves that you will take to reach checkmate, or at least capture one of your opponent's pieces.

If you are any good, you are also taking your opponent's countermoves into account and making contingency plans if they do not fall into your elaborately laid traps. In *Super Mario Bros.*, you are planning whether to take the higher path, which brings more reward but is riskier, or the safer lower path (figure 2.3). You are also planning to venture down that pipe that might bring you to a hidden treasure chamber, or to continue past it, depending on how much time you have left and how eager you are to finish the level. You may be planning to eat the power-up that lets you get through that wall so you can flick a switch that releases a bean from which you can grow a beanstalk that lets you climb up to that cloud you want to get to. In *Angry Birds*, you are planning where to throw each bird so as to achieve maximum destruction with the fewest birds. If you crush the ice wall with the blue bird, you can then hit that cavity with the black bomb bird, collapsing the main structure, and finish off that cowardly hiding pig with your red bird.

You think spatially. Chess takes place on a two-dimensional grid, where cells that are not occupied by white or black pieces are "empty." Those who have played the game a number of times and internalized its rules start seeing some of the opportunities and threats directly as they look at the board. The fact that the queen is threatened stands out like an X in a row of Os, and the possible positions a knight can go to are immediately visible on the board. In *Super Mario Bros.*, you need to estimate the trajectory of jumps to see whether you can pass gaps and bounce off enemies, which means seeing the jump in your mind's eye before you execute it. You also need to estimate whether you can get through that small aperture with your current size (Mario can change size) and whether that path over there leads anywhere. In *Angry Birds*, you also need to estimate trajectories, sometimes

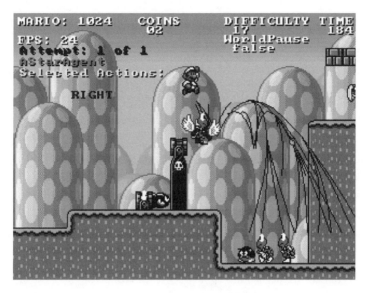

Figure 2.3
A planning algorithm (a version of the A* algorithm, discussed in chapter 4) playing a clone of *Super Mario Bros.* The black lines show the various future paths the algorithm is considering.

very complicated ones that involve bouncing and weird gravity, and you may also need to determine whether you can fit that bird in the narrow passage between that pixelated rock and that virtual hard place.

You predict the game and your opponent(s). In Chess, predicting what your opponent will do is essential to successful play. If you knew how your opponent would react to your moves, you could plan your strategies with perfect certainty that they would succeed. *Super Mario Bros.* and *Angry Birds* are usually not adversarial games (you are not playing against a human opponent), but instead the challenge is to predict the actions and reactions of the environment. When will the cannon fire? Which way will that turtle face if I land to the left of it? Will the monster lizard advance all the way if I don't jump up on the platform? And how exactly will that complex building collapse if I knock out the bottom support, where will all the pieces land, and will one of them set off that box of TNT to create a nice chain reaction? While randomness may play some role in *Angry Birds* (*Super Mario Bros.* is completely deterministic), the difficulty stems mainly from the very complex interactions among the various objects in the game.

You assess yourself. "Know yourself," said Socrates. He was probably not talking about Chess and certainly not about *Angry Birds*, but really, knowing yourself is an invaluable asset when playing games. Overestimating your skill will make you play recklessly and most likely lose; underestimating your skill means that you will not attempt that risky strategy that could have won the game for you. Also, you need to take your affect into account and correct for it. Are you currently off-balance because your plan did not work out, unhealthily buoyed by your recent success, or perhaps driven by lust for revenge for that bastard move your opponent just made to capture your queen? Well, then you need to take that into account. Don't try that ten-moves-deep strategy if you know it's based on wishful thinking rather than careful assessment of the situation. The same is true for *Super Mario Bros.* and *Angry Birds*: if you did not know your own skill level, you would not be able to progress in the game because you would try strategies that were too hard for you. You might also be better at executing some tactics, such as long jumps or setting traps with your knights, than others, such as precision shooting or moving in quickly to surround the king.

You move. It is true that Chess does not involve much in the way of motor skills, at least unless the game degenerates into a brawl, but the other two games certainly do. *Super Mario Bros.* has you pressing two keys and a D-pad, which is itself eight direction keys, very frequently (often multiple presses per second). *Angry Birds* demands very fine control of your finger movements on the screen in order to shoot the bird in the right direction with the right force and activate its special ability at the right time. In both games, these movements must be coordinated with what happens on screen and perfectly timed. It is the sensorimotor aspects of these games that tend to picked up very quickly by five-year-old kids but not always by their frustrated parents.

Of course, other games offer other challenges. First-person shooters such as *Halo* or *Call of Duty* challenge your spatial navigation in three dimensions, and in multiplayer modes, they throw you straight into the complexities of team strategy. Role-playing games such as *Skyrim* and *Mass Effect* require you to understand the motives behind the actions of complex characters, resolve ethical dilemmas, and navigate perilous politics (at least if you play them the way they are meant to be played— although you can get pretty far in some of them by just shooting everything that moves). Economic simulation games like *SimCity* and *Transport Tycoon* require you to understand and influence complex economical systems.

One way of trying to outline what types of cognitive challenges games offer is to look to psychology or, more precisely, psychometrics, to see if there is some handy list of cognitive abilities. We could then try to figure out how each of these abilities is required (or not) for playing games of different types. It turns out that there are indeed such lists. In particular, the Cattell-Horn-Carroll (CHC) theory divides general intelligence into eleven different "broad cognitive abilities," which are further subdivided into many more specialized cognitive abilities.[1] This taxonomy is based on statistical analysis of hundreds of different cognitive tests and is widely accepted in the psychometrics community (though as new empirical evidence comes in, categories are modified and added).

Table 2.1 lists the eleven broad cognitive abilities from CHC theory and gives some examples of situations in games where they are used. Note that this is very far from a complete list; I've more or less listed some of the first examples that came to mind, trying to get some diversity in terms of game genres. My guess is that almost any game would make use of at least five different cognitive abilities (*Super Mario Bros.*, *Angry Birds*, and Chess certainly do), but this is just a guess and I'm not aware of anyone having done research on it. Someone really should do that research.

In sum, we use many different forms of intelligence when we play games, more or less all the time. This sounds like a lot of hard work. It's amazing that playing games actually relaxes you, but it does. (I took several breaks to play games while writing this chapter.)

Do You Learn When Playing Games?

So far, we have discussed only the individual skills you exercise when you play a game. But you do not exercise them the same way all the time; you are building your skills as you play. It certainly does not feel as if you are taking a class while you are playing a game (if it does, it's not a very good game). Yet you learn. Here is proof: you are much better at the game after playing it for some time than you were when you started. Try playing one

Table 2.1
The various cognitive abilities according to Cattell-Horn-Carroll theory
and some examples of their use in games

Broad cognitive ability	Example use in games
Comprehension-knowledge	Communicating with other players in all manner of multiplayer games, from *Bridge* to *Gears of War* and *World of Warcraft*
Fluid reasoning	Combining evidence to isolate suspects in *Phoenix Wright*; solving puzzles in *Drop7*
Quantitative knowledge	Controlling complex systems involving lots of quantitative data, such as in *SimCity*, or character management in *Dungeons and Dragons*
Reading and writing ability	Reading instructions in games, following conversations, and selecting dialogue options in role-playing games such as *Mass Effect*; writing commands in text adventures such as *Zork*
Short-term memory	Everywhere! For example, remembering recently played cards in Texas hold'em poker or *Hearthstone*
Long-term storage and retrieval	Recalling previous games of Chess or *StarCraft* that resemble the current game to gain insights into strategy
Visual processing	Spotting the possible tile matches in *Candy Crush Saga* or the enemy snipers in *Call of Duty*
Auditory processing	Becoming aware of approaching zombies (and from which direction) in *Left 4 Dead*; overhearing secret negotiations in *Diplomacy*
Processing speed	Rotating pieces correctly in *Tetris*; micromanaging battles in *StarCraft*; playing speed Chess
Decision or reaction time/speed	Everywhere! For example, countering moves in *Street Fighter* or deciding what fruits to slice in *Fruit Ninja*

of the early levels in *Super Mario Bros.* or *Angry Birds* again. Or try playing a Chess computer at novice difficulty again, the one that beat you roundly the first time you tried. Piece of cake.

Raph Koster, a famous game designer, has made the argument that learning is the main reason games are fun.[2] Good games are designed to teach you how to play them; the better they teach you, the better designed they are. You have fun because you are learning to play the game, and when you stop learning, you stop having fun. If there is nothing more to learn, you grow tired of the game. Therefore, a trivial game that you can beat on your first attempt is not interesting, and neither is a near-impossible game that you cannot make any progress on. A well-designed game instead offers you a long, smooth difficulty progression where you can keep learning as you play. We can say that the game is *accessible* and *deep*.

For example, when you started playing *Super Mario Bros.*, you first had to learn what the buttons did—button A makes Mario jump and pressing the D-pad in different directions makes him walk left or right—and you then had to learn how to tackle the various challenges that the game presented. "So, there's a walking mushroom approaching. What can I do? Aha! I can jump on it!" As you progressed through the levels of *Super Mario Bros.*, you would have noticed that the challenges presented became trickier and trickier, but also that you were better and better prepared to handle them.

The oft-imitated design of *Super Mario Bros.*'s levels typically introduces a basic version of some challenge (say, a jump over a gap or an enemy caught in a valley between two pipes) and later presents more advanced versions of the same challenge (longer gaps, different kinds of enemies in the valley) or combinations of several earlier challenges (a long jump over a gap, after which you immediately land in a valley full of enemies). Every time, the completion of some previous challenges has prepared you for tackling the new, more advanced challenge. And after a while, when you thought that there were no ways left to produce new, interesting challenges by varying the existing challenges, the game throws in some new ingredient that offers further variation and deeper challenges. One such new ingredient, introduced rather late in the game, is the spiky enemy, which cannot be defeated by jumping on top of it. Adding spiky enemies to existing challenges forces you to develop new strategies to cope with the familiar-looking but fresh challenges. Finally, even when you've managed to finish the whole game (beating the boss at the last level and rescuing the princess), there is much left to discover, including hidden areas and treasures, and how to beat the whole game in under ten minutes (if you're of that persuasion). *Super Mario Bros.* is widely regarded as a masterpiece of game design, partly by virtue of being a masterpiece of pedagogics: a deep and rewarding course where the next improvement is always within reach.

The story is much the same for *Angry Birds*. First, you learn the basic motor skills of swiping your fingers to fling birds, before proceeding to understand how the various birds interact with the materials the towers are built from and which parts of the towers are most crucial to hit in order to raze the whole tower. Every once in a while, the game throws in new types of material, new birds, and other devices to expand the range of challenges. Even in Chess, the progression is similar, with the obvious exceptions that very little in the way of motor skills is necessary and that learning takes place over many games of Chess rather than on many levels of the same. First, you learn the basic rules of Chess, including how the pieces move and capture. Then you learn more advanced rules, which presuppose mastery of the simpler rules, including castling and when the game is a draw. You can then move on to learning heuristics,[3] first simple and then more advanced; then you learn opening books (lists of good opening moves), the quirks of particular players and playing styles, and so on.

The idea that playing (games or otherwise) goes hand in hand with learning is not unique to game design. The developmental psychologist Lev Vygotsky talks about "proximal zones of development" in children's play, where kids typically choose to play with objects and tasks that are just outside their capacities because these are the most rewarding.[4] Relatedly, the creativity theorist Mihaly Czikszentmihalyi's concept of *flow* states that flow can be experienced when performing a task that is so hard as to challenge you but not easy enough to bore you, and where the difficulty of the task increases as your performance improves. Czikszentmihalyi developed this concept in reference to artistic and scientific creativity, but it applies just as well to game playing.[5] From a seemingly completely different perspective, the machine learning researcher Jürgen Schmidhuber introduced a mathematical formalization of curiosity. In his model, a curious agent (human or artificial) goes looking for tasks that allow it to improve its model of the task, and therefore its capacity to perform the task.[6] In other words, according to Schmidhuber's theory, a mathematically optimally curious agent does the same thing as a young kid learning about the world by playing with it, or as a discerning player choosing to play games she likes or choosing challenges that seem interesting within that game.

To sum all this up, it seems that games challenge your brain in more than one way—way more than one way—and, furthermore, that good games are designed to keep you challenged by ramping up the challenge (and providing additional challenges) in a pedagogical manner. Schools should take note (some do). It is very likely that the good games, those that we choose to play and keep coming back to, are so good at least partly because they succeed in persistently challenging our brains in multiple ways.

So you definitely use your intelligence when you play games. At the same time, we saw in the previous chapter that it is possible to build software that can play Chess or Go better than any human while seemingly not being intelligent. So how come intelligence is needed for humans to play games, but not for machines to play them? What's going on here? It is time to try to nail down what we mean by *artificial intelligence* and, in the process, what we mean by *intelligence*.

3   What Is (Artificial) Intelligence?

This is already the third chapter of the book, but I have not yet defined what we are talking about. Let me try. *AI* is short for "artificial intelligence," and because "artificial" is a rather straightforward concept, we just need to define *intelligence*. There must be a good definition of intelligence around, right?

Well, the good news is that lots of people have defined *intelligence*. The bad news is that the definitions that have been proposed are quite different from each other and not very easy to reconcile at all. In fact, there are so many definitions that it is hard to even get an overview of all of them. This tells us two things: that the nature of intelligence is of central concern to many thinkers and that lots of work remains to be done. In this book, I present and make use of several different definitions of *intelligence*, and specifically *artificial intelligence*.[1] We'll start with what is perhaps the most famous conception of artificial intelligence.

Imagine you are chatting online with two people. Perhaps you're using Facebook messages, Twitter, Slack, SMS, or something else. If you're not into chatting—the very word might offend you as something that only millennials do—imagine that you are having a conversation with two people via text messages.

You might even be typing on sheets of paper on a typewriter and sending them back and forth in envelopes. The format doesn't matter. The important thing is that you are communicating in an old-fashioned text-only way with both people.

Now someone tells you that one of these people is in fact a machine—to be more precise, AI software running on a computer. The other is a human. Your task is to find out which is which or, if you want, who's who. You can ask both of your text partners anything you want, but they are not required to answer truthfully, especially if you ask whether they are a computer.

This test was proposed in 1950 by Alan Turing, whom we encountered in the first chapter.[2] (Mind you, this was before any actual general-purpose computers existed, much less Facebook and text messages, so Turing talked about "teleprinters.") Turing was addressing the question, "Can a machine think?" and proposed that one way of finding out was to see whether it could win at what he called "the imitation game" but has since come to be called the "Turing test."[3]

If the software is so good that you could not distinguish the human from the computer would that mean that it was intelligent? Try to imagine the situation. If you want to, you can imagine that the computer "won" the game not just once but multiple times. If it can outsmart you, it must surely be intelligent—unless you have an extremely low opinion about your own intelligence.

Some people just accept that if a computer could pass the Turing test, it would be intelligent. (Perhaps it needs to have passed it multiple times against multiple human judges; perhaps the judges need to be specially trained.[4]) Others, perhaps most, disagree. It becomes interesting when you ask people why the computer is not intelligent, even though it passes the Turing test.

Sadly, a not-uncommon answer is, "It can't be intelligent because it's a computer." Personally, I find it hard to answer this objection without sarcasm. But offending people is no way to conduct constructive discussion.

The best answer to the "it's only a computer" objection is to keep asking: "Why is it that a computer cannot be intelligent, whereas a human can?" Some people say that the word *intelligence* by definition applies only to humans. Okay, fine. Let's come up with another word then that means "intelligence" except it is not arbitrarily confined to humans. Others reply that the computer cannot be intelligent because it is made of silicon components like transistors, while a human is made out of living, biological cells. So why is it that having biological cells is necessary for intelligence? And how do you know? There are also those who claim that the computer could not be intelligent if it was programmed by humans; it must have learned by itself, perhaps by growing up with humans. Again, how do you know that intelligence can't be programmed? Have you tried? And how do you know that this particular computer program, which just fooled you into thinking it was a human, did not grow up with humans and go to school with the other kids? All you know about is that it was smarter than you.

There are a couple of good objections too. One is that communicating through written text is rather limited, and real humans communicate also through the tone of their voice, facial expressions, and body movements. Another is that this sort of interview situation is indeed a very unnatural one, and not really representative of the wide range of activities humans engage in every day. Some people handle a written interview situation terribly but are otherwise perfectly competent human beings. Conversely, being able to write eloquent answers to questions does not guarantee that you can get out of bed, tie your shoelaces, decide what you want to eat, comfort the ones you love, or paint a painting. Or play a game. Yet all of these activities seem to require intelligence of some kind.

Are Humans Intelligent?

As we can see, the Turing test is not without issues. But still, the basic idea of taking something that a human can do and task the computer with doing the same is appealing. It makes sense that if that a computer is truly intelligent, it should be able to do all those things that a human can do because of her intelligence.

However, this criterion makes at least two assumptions: that humans are indeed intelligent and that this is the only (or highest) type of intelligence. Humans appear to implicitly be the measure for intelligence just as for other things. So let's turn the question around and ask if, from the perspective of computers, humans are intelligent.

Humans would, compared to a computer, seem quite stupid in many ways. Let's start with the most obvious: humans can't count. Ask a human to raise 3,425 to the power of 542 and watch him sit there for hours trying to work it out. Ridiculous. The same goes for a number of other trivial tasks, such as calculating the average age in a population of 300 million. Shouldn't take more than a couple of seconds—unless you are a human, in which case it'll probably take you years, and even then you would have made a number of errors.

Humans have almost no memory either. Ask a human to give you the correct name and current address for a randomly chosen social security number (or personal registration number, or whatever the equivalent is in your country). Even if she has all the information in whatever format she prefers (such as a large paper catalog), it will still take her at least several seconds—and most humans would not even know where to get the information. Or ask a human to produce a hundred addresses to websites talking about artificial intelligence, or even a complete list of everything that happened to him yesterday. Humans talk about "goldfish memory," but from the perspective of a computer, the human and the goldfish aren't that far apart, capability-wise.

At this point, many readers will be protesting wildly and saying that I am being terribly unfair to them. I am only choosing tasks that computers excel at and ignoring those where humans have an advantage, such as motor control and pattern recognition.

Right. Computers can land a jet plane and fly a helicopter. In fact, almost any computer can do those things if you load the right software. Very few humans know how to land a jet plane, and even fewer know how to fly a helicopter. Many have the capacity to "load the software" (learn), but this is a process that takes years and is very expensive. Sometimes even trained humans fail spectacularly at these tasks. (It's hard to understand why anyone would want to be in a plane flown by a human now that there are alternatives.) Computers can drive regular cars on-road and off-road, obeying all traffic regulations. There are many humans who can't even do that.[5]

Speaking of pattern recognition, it's true that humans can recognize the faces of their friends with quite high accuracy. But then, humans have only a couple of hundred friends at most. The face recognition software that Facebook uses can tell the faces of hundreds of thousands of people apart. Other pattern recognition algorithms can successfully match a scan of a human thumb to the right fingerprint in a database of millions.

Now let's take another activity that humans should be good at: game playing. Games were invented by humans in order to entertain themselves, and because humans seem to find it entertaining to exercise their learning, motor, and reasoning capabilities, games should be perfectly tailored to human intelligence. Humans should excel at game playing, right? Well, not really. As we have seen, computers now totally own humans in basically all classic board games. And as we will see later, computers perform very well in many video games as well. There are still games where computers do better, though the development of better hardware and software means that computers are constantly closing the gap. You should also remember that all the games on which we compare humans and computers were designed by humans for humans. Therefore, they are particularly well suited to human cognitive strengths. It would be very easy to invent games that were so complicated that only computers could play them.[6] Computers could even invent such games themselves.

Other things that have been cited as pinnacles of human achievement are tying shoelaces and self-reproduction. But tying shoelaces is sort of pointless; it's getting to be an obsolete technology even for humans. Why would you need shoelaces if you're a robot? And humans don't really know how to reproduce themselves. They know how to have sex, which is quite a different thing and rather easy. The actual reproduction is down to various biochemical processes that humans don't completely understand yet and don't know how to replicate.

What about the Turing test, then? Well, the computers could define their own Turing test. They would probably define the interface so that instead of passing typed messages back and forth at a leisurely pace, it would take place over a 100 megabit per second optical cable. I do not think any human would do very well on this test.

So, compared to humans, computers seem to be doing quite well indeed—at least if you ask the computers. It all depends on what you measure.

Some humans would object that this comparison is absurd because it's humans who build and program computers. Therefore, any intelligence the computers have should be attributed to their human creators. But that is a dangerous argument for humans to make, because in that case, any intelligence that humans might have is not really their own but actually belongs to the process of evolution by natural selection that created them.

Doing What They Do on the Discovery Channel

Presumably, the last few pages have not convinced you that you are less intelligent than a computer. Clearly there was something missing from the discussion. There must be some kind of unspoken assumption that, when exposed, collapses the argument. I agree. Here is the problem:

All of the examples I gave were of computers being good (and humans bad) at performing very specific tasks and solving very specific problems, when the hallmark of real intelligence is to be able to perform well in a large variety of situations. Being very good at a single thing is never enough for intelligence. Therefore, humans are more intelligent than computers after all: a Chess-playing program cannot land a jet plane, and a face recognition program cannot play *Super Mario Bros.* or do exponentiation. Your intelligence is all about your ability to perform well in whatever situation you may find yourself, and humans are very good at adapting to a very wide range of situations and problems, whereas computer programs are usually suited only to the particular type of situation or problem they are programmed for.

Let us take a step back and think about what this means in some concrete situations for animals and for robots.

Ethology is the branch of biology that studies the behavior of animals and the mechanisms by which this behavior is produced—"animal psychology," you might call it. A central concept in this discipline is that of adaptive behavior—the behavior that an animal exhibits in response to the environment it was evolved in and which serves to increase its chances of surviving and having surviving offspring. It is easy to understand how it is adaptive for a fox to move so as to minimize its chances of detection when approaching the hare it hopes to make its dinner. Similarly, it is as easy to understand why it is adaptive for the hare to change directions at unpredictable intervals when trying to escape the faster but heavier fox whose dinner it does not want to be. What is not easy to understand is which of the fox and the hare is more intelligent. Indeed, for an ethologist, this question does not even make sense without first specifying what environment and what problem the animal is facing. Now and then you run into people (or tabloid newspapers) who claim that "dolphins are really as intelligent as humans" or "pigs are more intelligent than dogs" or similar nonsense. It's nonsense not because it is false but because it makes no sense to make such claims without first establishing the environment and life conditions in which intelligence is measured. Put a dolphin in an office chair, or a human in the ocean, and neither of them will see much success.

In the words of the great roboticist Rodney Brooks, "elephants don't play Chess." Brooks pioneered behavior-based robotics in the 1980s, an approach to robotics where computationally and mechanically simple robots were designed for coping with specific environments. For example, Brooks developed mechanical insects capable of following people around and avoiding walking into obstacles in indoor environments using only a couple of inexpensive motors and light sensors. Some of his robots had no actual computer at all, just some clever wiring between inputs and outputs. In contrast, most of the other robots of that time used state-of-the-art onboard computers and sophisticated sensors yet performed their tasks poorly and were very sensitive to any modification of the problem they were set out to solve, such as shadows shifting slightly because someone raised a shade. Very advanced and ambitious robots were failing at very simple tasks that simpler robots solved well. And this was precisely the point Brooks was making.

Elephants don't play Chess[7] because they don't need to. It's not adaptive for them. Why would they waste their precious brain capacity on this, and why would the elephants' genes waste space coding for them being able to learn to play Chess? In a similar way, Brooks showed that his robots could outperform many more advanced robot designs by throwing away all those extra layers of "general problem-solving capacity" and just getting on with solving whatever problem the robot was meant to solve by connecting the inputs almost directly to the outputs and devising some simple rules. It just seems to be much easier to design a robot that actually works that way. If you have ever worked in a large organization with multiple layers of management and bureaucracy, and observed how much more easily you could get things done if you just bypassed all that management and bureaucracy, you can probably relate.

Where does the notion of intelligence as adaptive behavior leave us with regard to the question of human intelligence and machine intelligence? One possible conclusion is that it is now meaningless to talk about whether a computer is intelligent "in general," just as it is meaningless to talk about whether an animal is intelligent in general. One can only ever talk about how well suited a computer program or an animal is to solving a particular problem or surviving in a particular environment.

But this is certainly a rather boring answer. It is also not a very useful one, at least not for artificial intelligence researchers who still want to cling to an idea that there is such a thing as "intelligence" that software (or humans, or animals) can have more or less of. Can we do better? Can we keep the idea of adaptive behavior and come up with a better definition of *intelligence*, and thus of *artificial intelligence*?

Getting Less Specific

Let's see if we can save the idea of intelligence while acknowledging that intelligence is always relative to some environment or task. This is what Shane Legg and Marcus Hutter, at the Swiss AI Institute IDSIA where I also worked for a while, attempted to do in an influential 2007 paper.[8] The basic idea of Legg and Hutter is that the *universal intelligence* of an agent (human, computer program, or something else) equals your ability to perform not only one task but many tasks—in fact, all possible tasks. But the simpler tasks are more important, and the more complex a task is, the less it weighs in the final summation.

This might need some explanation. What Legg and Hutter propose is an equation that in theory could be used to assign any agent (human, machine, or otherwise) a value between 0 and 1, where 0 means incapable of doing anything useful and 1 means perfectly, universally intelligent. The universal intelligence of the agent is defined as the sum of its performance over all possible tasks. Tasks are basically anything that an agent could fail or succeed on (predicting stock prices, tying shoelaces, making friends at a party). The agent's performance on each task is rewarded with a number between 0 and 1, where 0 is complete failure and 1 complete success. By dividing with the number of tasks, you get the agent's average performance on all tasks. In order to give more priority to the more fundamental tasks, those are weighted higher in the calculation; essentially, the importance of each task is inversely proportional to the shortest possible description of that task.

Are you still with me? Good. My description is rather technical, but the basic ideas can be summarized: (1) intelligence can be measured as your ability to solve problems and (2) you should measure intelligence over all possible problems, but (3) simpler problems (those that can be easily described) are more elementary and your ability to solve these should count more.

I think this makes a lot of sense. It might not accurately capture all the various meanings of the word *intelligence*, but I think it accurately captures one sense of intelligence that is very useful for developing artificial intelligence. You could define the search for artificial intelligence as the search for agents that have higher and higher universal intelligence.

It is not a practical measure, however. Actually, that's a bit of an understatement. You cannot test the universal intelligence of any given agent using the formula given by Legg and Hutter, because you need to test it on all possible tasks. But there are infinitely many tasks, and you don't have that much time. In addition, the shortest possible description of a task (the so-called

Kolmogorov complexity) is not computable. You cannot, even in theory, be sure that you have found the shortest description of a task. So to actually measure the intelligence of a program, we will have to look for something more practical.

Doing Better Than Humans

Defining *intelligence* in a way that is useful for artificial intelligence and at the same time true to our intuitive notion of intelligence seems to be far from easy. So maybe we should look at defining *artificial intelligence*—the activities and technology that are we typically refer to when using that term—without first trying to settle on a definition of intelligence. Let's be pragmatic. Versions of the following definition have been proposed by different people: "Artificial intelligence is the quest to make computers be able to do things that humans currently do better."

This is a refreshingly nonconstraining description. If we create a piece of software that understands human speech better than most humans do, that is progress in artificial intelligence. Creating software that can look at an X-ray of a human chest, diagnose the disease, and propose a course of treatment would also be progress in artificial intelligence. A self-driving car that obeys all traffic rules and avoids running over children who suddenly run out into the road? Definitely AI. And creating software that would beat a strong human player in a game such as *StarCraft* or *DOTA* would certainly count as progress in AI.

However, isn't this definition a bit too wide? Imagine that you invented an artificial liver. (You would become rich!) Cleansing the blood is something that we currently can't do very well with artificial systems; actually, livers are the only devices that can do it well. That's why you need a liver transplant to survive if the one liver that your body came with gets messed up. However, it feels very weird to say that creating an artificial liver would represent progress in artificial intelligence. It's more like a solving a chemical problem, isn't it?

One could argue that in order to be artificial intelligence, the technology needs to be able to do something that humans do better *consciously*. I don't know about you, but I'm certainly not conscious of what my liver is doing right now. I'm not conscious of how I understand spoken language either, and I'm only partly conscious of the strategies I employ when I play Chess or the action adventure game *Bloodborne*.

Another issue, or perhaps feature, with this definition is that it includes *narrow AI*. It is entirely possible to imagine a system that drives perfectly in city traffic or one that issues better diagnoses of chest diseases than any doctor, but makes no progress whatsoever toward more general AI—no progress toward something that would, for example, pass a Turing test.

The distinction between narrow AI and general AI (or artificial general intelligence—AGI, as some call it) is important for another reason. Occasionally you might hear people say that "AI has failed." Researchers have been working on AI since the 1950s, but there is still no Robocop, HAL, or Wall-E around or even something that could pass the Turing test. From the perspective of general AI, it is true that we have not yet produced AI. However, it took much more than fifty years from the invention of paper kites until the Wright brothers built the first self-powered flying machine,[9] including hundreds of years of technical developments of wheels, engines, theory, and materials. And you could certainly say that there has been plenty of technical development in AI since the 1950s.

From the perspective of narrow AI, the claim that AI has failed is utterly false. Much of the technology you use every day and that our society is built on started as AI research. The image recognition software in your phone camera that helps you take better photos, the voice processing algorithms in your personal assistant software, your GPS navigator that finds the shortest route to the concert venue, and of course the creepy suggestions from Facebook about who you should add as a friend: it is all the result of AI research. In fact, the object-oriented programming style of programming that most software you use is programmed in, and the relational database model that almost every website uses also started as research into how to make machines truly intelligent. It could be argued that reproducing intelligence was one of the driving forces for the original inventors of the computer. However, it seems that as soon as AI research produces something that actually works and is useful, it's spun off into its own research field and is no longer called artificial intelligence.

From this perspective, it would be only slightly irreverent to define *artificial intelligence* as any ambitious computer technology that doesn't quite work yet.

So, What *Is* (Artificial) Intelligence?

You might be forgiven for running out of patience at this point. I've spent this entire chapter bouncing from one definition of *intelligence* and *artificial intelligence* to another, seemingly finding shortcomings in each. I started with describing the Turing test as a test and implicitly a definition of artificial intelligence, but concluded that it doesn't test for lots of things that a normal human being does and which seem to require intelligence (cooking, tying your shoelaces, a knowing smile), and that it would thus be possible for a rather unintelligent being to pass the test. Also, the test is highly dependent on the particular human interrogator; some humans might fail to spot an obvious AI, and we don't want the definition of whether a machine is actually intelligent to depend on frail human judgment. Next, we discussed the idea of intelligence as adaptive behavior, where intelligence would be something completely different depending on the environment an agent (a surgeon, a sturgeon, a vacuuming robot) lives in. But this sort of evades the question and does not allow us to say that one agent is more intelligent than another. So we then considered the idea that universal intelligence is the average performance of an agent on all possible problems, weighted by the simplicity of the problems. This makes sense theoretically but is impossible to measure in practice. Finally we discussed the idea that AI is simply about trying to create software (and occasionally hardware) that tries to do things than humans currently do better than computers.

The truth is that there is no commonly agreed definition of either of these concepts, and even experts frequently talk about intelligence and artificial intelligence with different implicit meanings depending on the context. We'll just have to live with it. So in the rest of this book, I will *use artificial intelligence* to mean either of the following things, depending on what I am talking about:

1. The quest to build intelligent machines, for some definition of intelligence.

2. Whatever people who call themselves artificial intelligence researchers do.

3. A set of algorithms and ideas developed by artificial intelligence researchers. The minimax and MCTS algorithms from

chapter 2 are good examples of AI algorithms, and I will present more such algorithms in coming chapters.

Finally, what did Alan Turing—inventor of the Turing test and arguably the first person to pose several key problems in AI—think? Well, contrary to what many believe, Turing did not propose what is now known as the Turing test as a definition of artificial intelligence; instead, he proposed it to show that our whole concept of intelligence was flawed and that there was no point in arguing about whether some machine was intelligent. Turing thought that we would eventually develop software that would pass the test he had invented, but that "the original question, 'Can machines think?' I believe to be too meaningless to deserve discussion."[10]

4 Do Video Games Have Artificial Intelligence?

Many, perhaps most, video games feature so-called nonplayer characters (NPCs). These could be adversaries, allies, bystanders, or something else. The point is that they are controlled not by the player (you) but by the computer. Usually people refer to the way these NPCs behave as the "AI" of the game.

As we have established that there are many different views on what artificial intelligence is, let us simply accept that moniker for whatever controls the NPCs in video games. But how exactly does the AI in a typical video game work? Behold a little dramatization.

Seven Seconds in the Life of Enemy 362

Enemy 362 spawned 43 minutes into the game session. The game had already spawned 361 enemies in this play session; the player had killed 143 of these, and the others had simply expired when the player left the zone of the game in which they existed. The player had made her way into the third level of this rather generic first-person shooter (FPS) (I think of it as something like a *Call of Duty* game, but it could also be something like *Gears of War*, or *Half-Life*), and her character was now single-handedly

Figure 4.1

First person-shooters are so called because you view the world from a first-person perspective and, well, shoot things. *Call of Duty: Modern Warfare 2* (Infinity Ward, 2009) is a good representative of the genre.

assaulting the hideout of an infamous international terrorist (see figure 4.1). Enemy 362, looking like a typical lower-rank terrorist with ragged combat fatigues, a black scarf covering the lower half of its face, and a Kalashnikov assault rifle, was tasked with failing to protect the terrorist boss at the end of the level. Unless the player really messed up, of course.

As always—in every game session—enemy 362 spawned at the same place, next to the abandoned-looking hut, as soon as the player passed the third checkpoint of the level. When enemy 362 came into existence, its mind was in state 0. This is how the mind of enemy 362 looks:

- *State 0: Guard.* Slowly walk back and forth between the abandoned hut where it spawned and the palm tree, looking back and forth. If the player character appears within the field of vision, go to state 1.

- *State 1: Take cover.* Run as fast as possible to the nearest cover point. A pile of sandbags are suitably located between the abandoned hut and the palm tree. When cover is reached, go to state 2.
- *State 2: Stay in cover.* Stay crouched behind cover so as to be as hard to hit as possible. Set a timer for a random amount between 1 and 3 seconds. When that amount of time has passed, go to state 3. If at any point the player character advances beyond the point of cover, go to state 4.
- *State 3: Fire from cover.* Stand up behind cover and fire at the player character, with a random deviation of 5 degrees so as not hit too often. Set a timer for either 1 or 2 seconds. When that time has passed, go to state 3. If at any point the player character advances beyond the point of cover, go to state 4.
- *State 4: Attack player.* Run straight toward the player along the shortest path, firing continuously at the player.
- *State 5: Die.* If at any point health is reduced to 0, fall down on the ground and do nothing more.

The architecture of enemy 362's mind is called a *finite state machine.* This is because it is organized as a finite number of states,[1] where each state contains instructions for how to behave in that state. Incidentally, all of the NPCs in this game share this architecture, but the different types of enemies differ in which particular states they have.

In states 1 and 4, enemy 362 is running toward a position. This is accomplished using the A^* algorithm, which is a path-finding algorithm. In other words, it is a method for finding the shortest path from point A (for example, where a character is standing) to point B (for example, behind some sandbags). A^* works as follows:

1. Start at point A, the starting position, and select this as the active position.

2. Look at all the positions next to the active position and find out which ones are possible to go to (they are not, for example, inside a wall). In this example, it might look at eight points in a circle with a diameter of half a meter around the active position.

3. Those positions that are possible to go to are added to a list of available positions, which is sorted according to how far they are to the goal (point B) along a straight line.

4. Select the position that is closest to the goal[2] from this list, and remove it from the list. (The other points are kept in the list.) Mark this point as the active position. Go to step 2.

Essentially the algorithm keeps track of a large number of positions, and constantly explores the most promising one. Running this process will always result in finding the shortest path between point A and point B, and usually it will find it pretty quickly—much faster than if it had investigated all possible positions in the area. (There are some further complexities to the algorithm, but these are not necessary to discuss to give you a general idea of it.)

The finite state machine architecture and the A* algorithm play central roles in most games and are also used widely in robotics and self-driving cars. Many games use additional algorithms on top of this to control NPC behavior, and some do not use any of these techniques (in recent years, an alternative to finite state machines, called behavior trees, has become popular). But it's fair to say that finite state machines and A* are among the most common algorithms for implementing NPC behavior in commercial video games.[3]

So let us return to enemy 362. After suddenly finding itself in the world, it dutifully starts walking from the hut to the palm tree. It gets only halfway there, though, before it spots the player character advancing toward it. It goes into state 1 for only a fraction of a second because it is already next to the sandbags. It goes to state 2 for a few seconds and then to state 3, standing up and firing straight at the player character. However, the player character has hidden behind cover of her own and is not hit. Enemy 362 goes back to state 1 while the player character lobs a grenade. The force of the explosion instantly depletes all health, causing a rapid transition to state 5.

Enemy 362 did not have a name and is quickly forgotten by the player as she advances further. There would not normally be anyone to write the biography of enemy 362, for in truth there is not much to remember. The flip side of this is that nobody would feel any guilt for dispensing with enemy 362 so quickly. It's not like there was any actual mind to put an end to.

Is This Really All There Is?

You may note that after pulling back the curtain on the Wizard of Oz, there are only smoke and mirrors after all—some pretty impressive smoke and well-polished mirrors, but still. Of course, the actual implementation of NPC control in any given game is much more complex than what I have explained, but the principles are very similar.

You might also notice everything that's missing. The AI controlling enemy 362 is not a complete mind in any way. It cannot do anything other than what is recorded in those five states. If you hide behind a wall for an hour, enemy 362 will keep transitioning between states 2 and 3 until you come out. It will not decide that it has had enough and proceed to flank you instead or call on its friends for help.

It's true that there are examples of more interesting NPCs in some existing games, even among first-person shooters. For example, the horror-themed shooter *F.E.A.R.* introduced the use of planning algorithms in modern action games. Using planning, enemies could coordinate their attacks and do such things as flanking the player; the player could also overhear the chatter between enemies to try to second-guess their plans. The *Halo* series of first-person shooters has also shown how more engaging NPC behavior can be implemented; for example, enemies often move in squads, some enemies retreat when others are killed, and some enemies will try to guess where you will appear if you try hiding from them. A more recent example is *Shadow of Mordor*, a game where NPCs remember their encounters with you and refer back to them in future fights.[4]

Still, these examples are pretty much the state of the art—at least for this type of game—and each of the advances could be described as a very specific trick rather than an advancement in general-purpose AI. Just like our fictive enemy 362 from a fictive generic first-person shooter, the NPCs of even the most sophisticated games are limited in the forms of behavior they can express and the forms of interaction they can understand. Here is a *very* partial list of things that enemy 362 cannot do:

- Figure out that you were hiding behind a wall for an hour instead of assaulting it, and so consider alternative options, such as flanking you.
- Throw pebbles at you until you move from behind that wall.
- Call for backup.
- Feel fear.

- Have a philosophical conversation with you, shouted across that wall, about the meaning of war and why you and it are fighting each other.
- Propose, and play, a nice game of Chess with you instead.
- Tie its shoes.
- Make a cup of decent coffee.

Of course, it is entirely possible to write code that would allow enemy 362 to do each of these things—except, perhaps, feeling fear.[5] Indeed, some games include NPCs that flank you, throw pebbles at you, hold (scripted) philosophical conversations with you, and so on. But each of these capacities has to be built specifically by a human designer. Someone would have to specifically write the program code that makes it possible for enemy 362 to throw pebbles (maybe add a few states to the finite state machine and an algorithm for figuring out where to throw the pebbles), or write the lines in the philosophical discussion that you would be able to choose to engage in, complete with an interface where you can select your responses. If enemy 362 is to be able to put the AK47 away and pull out a Chess board to play with you, the game developers need to implement a minimax algorithm to act as enemy 362's Chess brain and, of course, the graphics and interface elements to allow playing Chess. None of these capabilities will emerge magically from the AI of enemy 362 because, as we saw, its "brain" is just a finite state machine and a pathfinding algorithm.

At this point, I would like to contrast what I just told you with the wild imagination I had when I was eleven years old and played games on my Commodore 64, as I related in the prologue. I kept fantasizing about what would happen if I played the games in ways beyond which I could: of sailing beyond the edge of the map in *Pirates!*, of taking control of (or just talking to) individual people in a strategy game such as *Civilization*, or bringing my favorite characters from other games into *Bubble Bobble*. Basically, I fantasized that games were infinite and had room for infinite possibilities.

Another way of seeing this is that I imagined that interacting with games could have something like the amazing possibility space of interacting with a human being or even a cat or a dog. You are reading this book now and thinking thoughts that you never thought before, following along with my argument or perhaps formulating counterarguments of your own. Your reactions are likely to surprise me, or at least I would not be able to predict them. Could games not be the same?

You might expect that I—an adult and professor who has published hundreds of articles about artificial intelligence, in particular about artificial intelligence and games—have overcome these childhood fantasies and adopted a more sober view. Well, no. Far-fetched fantasy scenarios are necessary for scientific progress. So let me present you with one vision of what it would be like to have games that more thoroughly built on AI methods.

What If Video Games Had Actual AI?

Let's step into the future and assume that many of the various AI techniques we are working on at the moment have reached perfection and we could make games that use them. In other words, let's imagine what games would be like if we had good enough AI for anything we wanted to do with AI in games. Imagine that you are playing a game of the future.

You are playing an open world game—in other words, a game in which you roam a relatively open space and pursue game objectives in any order you choose. (Examples of popular open-world game series include *Grand Theft Auto*, *The Elder Scrolls*, and *The Legend of Zelda*) In this hypothetical future open world game, you decide that instead of going straight to the next mission objective in the city you are in, you feel like driving (or riding) five hours in some randomly chosen direction. West, maybe. The game makes up the landscape as you go along, and you end up in a new city that no human player has visited before. In this city, you can enter any house (though you might have to pick a few locks), talk to everyone you meet, involve yourself in a completely new set of intrigues, and carry out new missions. If you had gone in a different direction, you would have reached a different city with different architecture, different people, and different missions—or a huge forest with realistic animals and eremites, or a secret research lab, or whatever else the game engine comes up with.

Talking to these people you find in the new city is as easy as just talking to the screen. The characters respond to you in natural language that takes into account what you just said. These lines are not read by an actor but generated in real time by the game. You could also communicate with the game though waving your hands around, dancing, or facial expressions or other exotic modalities. Of course, in many (most?) cases, you are still pushing buttons on a keyboard or controller because that is often the most efficient way of telling the game what you want to do.

It is perhaps needless to say, but all NPCs navigate and generally behave in a thoroughly believable way. For example, they will not get stuck running into walls or repeat the same sentence over and over (well, not more than an ordinary human would). This also means that you have interesting adversaries and collaborators to play any game with without having to resort to waiting for your friends to come online or have to resort to being matched with annoying thirteen-year-olds.

Within the open world game, there are other games to play, for example, by accessing virtual game consoles within the game world or proposing to play a game with some NPC. These NPCs are capable of playing the various subgames at whatever level of proficiency that fits with the game fiction, and they play with human-like playing styles. It is also possible to play the core game at different resolutions, for example, as a management game or as a game involving the control of individual body parts, by zooming in or out. Whatever rules, mechanics, and content are necessary to play these subgames or derived games are invented by the game engine on the spot. Any of these games can be lifted out of the main game and played on its own.

The game senses how you feel while playing the game and figures out which aspects of it you are good at, as well as which parts you like (and, conversely, which parts you suck at and despise). Based on this, the game constantly adapts itself to be more to your liking, for example, by giving you more stories, challenges, and experiences that you will like in that new city that you reached by driving five hours in a randomly chosen direction—perhaps by changing its own rules. It's not just that the game is giving you more of what you already liked and mastered. Rather more sophisticatedly, the game models what you preferred in the past and creates new content that responds to your evolving skills and preferences as you keep playing.

Although the game you are playing is endless, is of infinite resolution, and continuously adapts to your changing tastes and capabilities, you might still want to play something else at some point. So why not design and make your own game? Maybe because it's hard and requires lots of work? Sure, it's true that back in 2018, it required hundreds of people working for years to make a high-profile game and a handful of highly skilled professionals to make any notable game at all. But now that it's the future and we have advanced AI, this can be used not only inside the game but also in the game design and development process, so you simply switch the game engine to edit mode and start sketching a game idea—a bit of a storyline here, a character there, some mechanics over here, and a set piece on top of it. The game engine immediately fills in the missing parts and provides you with a complete, playable game. Some of it is suggestion. If you have sketched an in-game economy but the economy is imbalanced and will lead to rapid inflation, the game engine will suggest a money sink for you, and if you have designed gaps that the player character cannot jump over, the game engine will suggest changes to the gaps or to the jump mechanic. You can continue sketching, and the game engine will convert your sketches into details, or jump right in and start modifying the details of the game. Whatever you do, the game engine will work with you to flesh out your ideas into a complete game with art, levels, and characters. At any time, you can jump in and play the game yourself. You can also watch any number of artificial players play various parts of the game, including players that play like you would have played the game or like your friends (with different tastes and skills) would have played it.

Why Is the Future Not Here Yet?

Why do we not already have something like what I just described? Because we don't have the technology yet and because game design and development practices are not very good yet at integrating the AI technology we have.

Let us start with the second reason. Artificial intelligence is on everyone's lips these days, and advances in AI methods are published almost daily. Yet the game industry has seemed curiously uninterested in incorporating most AI techniques in their games. Many academic AI researchers have proposed new AI algorithms for games and excitedly presented them to game developers, only to see said game developers explain (in a more or less polite manner) how the new algorithm is pointless to them. Sometimes this can be attributed to AI researchers' not understanding games or to game developers' not understanding AI, but most often this is because the games industry just doesn't work that way.

Essentially, the games industry is confined by economic realities to be highly risk averse and rather shortsighted. Big-budget video games typically take one to three years to develop and may involve hundreds of professionals during this time; it often consumes most or all resources of a single studio. At the same time, the games market is hit-driven, with mediocre games making very little money. So the game has to be a hit or the studio goes bust. Deadlines are tight, so the technology needs to be certain to work. Because so many game development studios don't know whether they will be around after they release their next game, they typically have little in the way of research or long-term development.

Under these conditions, some new AI technology that might work wonders, but also may be very hard to work with, is not an easy sell to most game developers. Instead, games are designed around existing and proven technologies, such as the finite state machine and pathfinding that makes up the brain of enemy 362. Games are designed to not need (nontrivial) AI. We will return to the question of why games are designed around the lack of AI and what can do about this in Chapter 9.

Now on to the first reason that the future is not here yet. Of course we don't have games like the one I envisioned because we don't have the technology yet. Currently, our mature AI techniques mostly allow for solutions to well-defined computational problems. It is very hard to build AI that can deal with situations that are not carefully defined, almost scripted. The kind of AI that can deal with emergent situations, learning and adapting, is to a large extent still on the drawing board.

And let us not forget that for some types of games, the limited capabilities of current artificial intelligence method fall short even for the most narrowly defined problems. Take strategy games—for example, any game in the *Civilization* series of turn-based epic strategy games. In these games, you guide a civilization from the Neolithic age to the space age, meanwhile engaging in exploration, expansion, warfare, and research. Similarly to other strategy games, at any given point you typically have a large number of "units" (military or otherwise) scattered around the world, and you need to tell them all what to do. Compare that to Chess, or Go, or Checkers, where you only move or place one unit every turn. The fact that you have so many units at the same time in a game such as *Civilization* means that the number of possible moves quickly gets astronomical (figure 4.2). If you have one unit that you can move to ten different places (or generally take ten different actions with), you have a branching factor of 10; if you have two units, you have a branching factor of 10 * 10 = 100; three units, 10 * 10 * 10 = 1000 ... We quickly reach branching factors of millions and even billions.

Figure 4.2
The games in the *Civilization* series (Firaxis, 1991–2016) allow you to
lead a civilization through thousands of years of expansion, research,
diplomacy, and war. The possibility space is quite overwhelming for
computers and humans alike.

Under such circumstances, algorithms such as minimax
quickly break down. There are simply too many potential actions
to consider, and the search can hardly begin looking at the con-
sequences of each. This is the reason that *Civilization*, which
is primarily a single-player game,[6] is infamous for its "bad AI";
computer-controlled units rarely coordinate with each other and
generally appear stupid. To offer a competitive challenge, the
game has to "cheat" by effectively conjuring units out of thin
air where the player is not looking. Similar situations occur in
other strategy games. The real-time strategy game *StarCraft* is a
favorite for competitive play between humans, and there have
been competitions between AI players since 2010. Despite all the

efforts, the best *StarCraft*-playing AI barely plays better than a human beginner player. The complexity of the game—the number of actions available to take with repercussions on different timescales—simply overwhelms our current AI methods.[7]

So far, we have only looked at work on using AI to play games or control the characters in games (two closely related tasks, though not the same). As we saw in chapter 2, there has been work on using AI to play classic board games since before there were computers; recently, more and more researchers have started working on AI that can play video games and new approaches to creating interesting nonplayer character behavior. But AI methods can be used for much more than this. If we are going to realize the vision of AI-driven games we just discussed, we will need AI that can adapt its behavior, learn from previous failures and successes, understand what the player knows and likes, create new levels and games, and work with us on designing experiences. In the next few chapters, we will explore some recent attempts at inventing AI that can do these things.

5 Growing a Mind and Learning to Play

So far in this book, you have read about a couple of different types of algorithms that can be used to play a game in some sense —in particular, the minimax algorithm for board game playing in chapter 2 and the finite state machines and A* search for FPS bots in chapter 4. These algorithms are designed by humans and integrated by humans into the complex software systems we call video games. Building such systems is often what creating AI is about: assembling various components (algorithms) so that they support each other, tuning them to work well in concert, testing how the final product works, and then going back and redoing things—like you would build a bike, a water pump. or an electronic circuit. Constructing such AI is a craft and a relatively pedestrian activity that does little to appeal to the romantic mind drunk on the promise of artificial intelligence that learns on its own and decides for itself.[1] Also, and perhaps more important, it's a labor-intensive and therefore expensive process that any game developer (or anyone else depending on some degree of artificial intelligence in her product) would love to see automated.

The idea of an AI that develops itself so that you don't have to program it—just tell it what sort of thing it should learn to do well—sounds a lot more appealing than hand-coding AI to an AI romantic, as well as to a business-minded person focusing on the financial bottom line. So let's find out how it can be done. One way is to try to create AI systems the way we ourselves were made: through Darwinian evolution.

A Very Simple Idea

The idea of evolution by natural selection seems utterly unremarkable and almost self-evident to most people in modern Western societies. But just over 150 years ago, when Charles Darwin published *The Origin of Species*, it was radical, heretical, and dangerous.[2] It was also far from obvious to everybody that it worked or even made sense. Because the core ideas of evolution by natural selection can easily become mixed up with all kinds of other ideas, let's try to boil the concept down to its bones to see whether we can reproduce it in a computer.

For evolution to work, you need three ingredients: variation, (imperfect) heredity, and selection. *Variation* means that there should be some difference among individuals. This implicitly assumes that there are things called individuals—we have not gone into detail on what these are yet—and that there's more than one individual. The set of all individuals is called a "population." *Heredity* means that the individuals can reproduce, either on their own or together with other individuals, and that the offspring resulting from this reproduction somehow resemble their "parents." Generally it's assumed that the heredity is not perfect, so that the offspring are not identical clones of their parents; if the population is small and parents can reproduce asexually without mixing with other parents, this condition becomes necessary. Finally, *selection* simply means that some individuals get to have more offspring than others, for some reason. We say that individuals that get to have more offspring are more "fit" than the other; an individual's "fitness" can be approximated by how many grandchildren that individual gets to have.

Let's consider this in the context of rabbits. First, we have variation. All rabbits are different from each other, and even if you or I cannot tell the difference between one rabbit and another, they presumably can themselves. Some of this variation is functionally meaningful; for example, some rabbits might have longer legs so they can run faster and others have sharper eyes so they can spot foxes at a greater distance. Then, we have heredity. The blueprint for a rabbit, as for all other animals and plants, is in its DNA. Rabbits (frequently) practice sexual reproduction (after all, they breed like rabbits) resulting in the DNA from one rabbit recombined with that of another. There are typically also some small changes introduced to the DNA in each generation; these are due to transcription errors when the DNA string is copied in the cell division process and are called *mutations*. Finally we have selection. This can happen in many ways—I know very little about what makes rabbits attractive to each other—but an obvious form of selection is that rabbits that get caught by a fox do not get to have as many offspring as those who outrun it. Selection is dependent not only on the individual rabbit but also on the rest of the population: to outrun the fox, you don't actually have to be faster than the fox, you just have to be faster than some other rabbit. Therefore, every small improvement to running speed, evasion tactics, or eyesight could mean a higher fitness for a rabbit. Over very many generations of rabbits, we get very good rabbits, or at least rabbits that are good at outrunning foxes.

Of course, foxes are also subject to evolution through natural selection. While variation and heredity are very similar for the fox population and the rabbit population, selection works somewhat differently. Foxes that fail to catch rabbits ultimately starve and cease their foxhood without reproducing, whereas those that catch and eat rabbits might acquire sufficient nutrients for surviving and having offspring. Of course, whether a fox catches a rabbit depends on both the fox and the rabbit (and possibly the other rabbits in the same herd). So the fitness of the fox is coupled to the fitness of the rabbit in a process known as *coevolution*; the fox population and the rabbit population enter an "arms race" where the foxes develop better and better tactics and bodily features for pursuing rabbits, and rabbits develop better and better ways of evading foxes. After many generations of rabbit and fox coevolution, some rabbits are still caught by foxes and most still escape. But if a rabbit from a thousand generations back meets a latest-generation shiny new fox, the fox is almost certain to win, and vice versa. Coevolutionary arms races are responsible for a range of fascinating phenomena in nature, including the extreme speeds of cheetahs and gazelles, the long beaks of hummingbirds, and the peculiar shape of the flowers which the hummingbirds pollinate, that hides their valuable nectar deep within the flower.

But this chapter is not going to literally be about the birds and the bees. I promised to talk about how to grow a mind, so let us see how evolution could apply to computer programs. First, we have variation. Imagine a population of different computer programs; they differ in their source code, so they also differ in what they do. In the simplest case, these programs are all random in the beginning. Then we have heredity. We can make offspring from a program by simply copying it, and then make the heredity imperfect by introducing a few mutations (changing a few small pieces of the source code). We could also combine the source code from two parent programs, taking some pieces from one and some from the other, to create an offspring program in a process known as *crossover*. Finally, we come to selection. We simply measure how good the programs are at what they do and assign higher fitness to those that perform some task better. The task could be anything you want a computer program to do: sort a list, paint a picture, perhaps play a game. Based on this fitness measurement, we simply throw away the bad programs and make mutated or recombined copies of the good ones. It's a code-eat-code world in there!

Does this makes sense to you? If it doesn't, you have my full understanding. It is a bit hard to believe initially that we can evolve programs because there are good arguments as to why it should not work. Random programs, for example, are not likely to be very good at anything at all; in fact, they will likely not even run. So how could you give a population of worthless computer programs any sensible fitness values? As for mutation, introducing random changes to a program will most likely just make it worse, probably even break it so it won't work at all. It is hard to see how this could make programs better at all.

And yet evolution does work, not only in nature but also in the computer. *Evolutionary algorithms*, as algorithms based on the principles of evolution by (artificial) selection are called, are frequently used for tasks as diverse as forecasting financial time series, controlling jet engines, and designing radar antennas. Also, some of the best game-playing AIs are at least partly constructed by evolution, as we shall see. In order to help understand how it is that this unlikely process actually works, it helps to consider the following.

First, while it is true that randomly constructed programs will usually be extremely bad at solving any given task, it's not necessary that any of the programs actually solve the task they are given. All we need to get evolution started is a way of distinguishing which of the programs are a little less worthless at solving their task—which of them mess it up the least—and select those for reproduction. Over sufficiently many generations, the programs can then move from atrocious to almost hopeless to merely bad to half-bad to okay to rather good to good to excellent. But in order for this to happen, we need a *fitness function*, a way of assigning fitnesses to programs, that can capture all these nuances. This is one reason games are great for AI research: it is usually easy to measure the performance of a player very precisely through score or ranking against other player. I describe later in this chapter how a good fitness function helped me evolve racing game drivers that drive better than I do.

Second, it is true that random changes to a program written in a standard programming language like Java, Python, or C++ are likely to destroy the program; most code changes result in the program not running at all, just like removing a single random stick in a Jenga tower will likely lead the tower to collapse, or removing a single random piece in a Chess game in an advanced state of play will alter the game balance completely. But we don't need to use these languages when we evolve programs. Choosing a correct *representation* for your programs is a very important part of making evolution work. For many types of programs, we now have representations where most small mutations to the program are not disastrous, and many are actually beneficial for the fitness of the program. In particular, a good way of representing these programs is as neural networks.

A Very Small Brain

Like so many other concepts within artificial intelligence, you can see (and talk about) neural networks from romantic or pragmatic perspectives. From a romantic perspective, neural networks are little brain simulators, imitating the core functionality of the brain's neural circuitry. From a pragmatic perspective, neural networks are just nonlinear equation systems, implementing geometric transformations on input data.

Figure 5.1 illustrates a simple neural network. It is organized into four layers: an input layer (with six nodes), two hidden

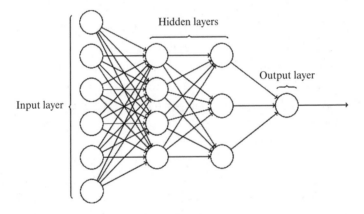

Figure 5.1
This figure illustrates a very simple neural network. It is organized into four layers: an input layer (with six nodes), two hidden layers (with four and three neurons each), and an output layer (with only one neuron). Each node (often called a "neuron" by analogy to biological neurons in brains) belongs to a particular layer and is connected to all neurons in the next layer. This type of neural network is called a feedforward network, because values are fed (or propagated) forward from one layer to the next.

layers (with four and three neurons each), and an output layer (with only one neuron). Each node (often called "neuron" by analogy to biological neurons in brains) belongs to a particular layer and is connected to all neurons in the next layer. This type of neural network is called a *feedforward network*, because values are fed (or propagated) forward from one layer to the next.

You use a feedforward neural network by assigning ("inputting") values, called activations, to the neurons in the input layer. These activations are then propagated to the next layer via the connections between the neurons, and the connections have values (called "weights") themselves. When an activation passes from one neuron to another, it is multiplied by the weight of the connection between neurons. Because all neurons in one layer connect to all neurons in the next layer, the activation of a cell in some layer (e.g., the first hidden layer) is the sum of all neuron activations in the previous layer (e.g., the input layer) multiplied by the weights of the connections from that layer. And then all this happens again when passing activations to the next layer. And so on.

If the idea that lots of neuron activations, which are really just numbers, are multiplied by other numbers doesn't clarify anything, try thinking of the neural network like a system of pipes.[3] Some kind of liquid (say, rum) is fed into the input layer and then passed on from neuron through neuron through pipes of varying diameter. The thicker pipes naturally carry more liquid, so neurons with thick pipes from high-activation neurons receive more liquid and are able to pass on more of it. Thickness of pipes here corresponds to weight of connections.

It's almost that simple, but there is one more important detail: every time the activation for a neuron has been computed, it passes through a nonlinear function (such as the hyperbolic tangent or the rectified linear function). This improves the computational capacity of the neural network but understanding it is not really essential to understanding what happens on a conceptual level. Apart from that, it really is that simple. At least the basics are. The basic idea of activations being passed from neurons through connections of varying weights is the same in almost all types of neural networks, even those that have connections that vary in strength, loop back on themselves, and share weights with other connections. Even the very large networks that are used in what is nowadays called "deep learning" and that might have dozens of layers and millions of connections are at their core just equation systems or, if you prefer, systems of pipes.

These simple computational constructs are surprisingly useful and versatile; mathematically speaking, a sufficiently large network can approximate any function. Neural networks can be taught to recognize faces, drive cars, compose music, translate text, and so on. Yes, they can also be taught to play games. But first they need to be taught, or *trained*, meaning that all the connection weights need to be set. Because the connection weights define what the neural network can do, the same neural network structure with different connection values could be good at doing completely different things, such as conjugating French verbs, playing football, or finding defects in steel sheets. And a neural network with random connection weights is usually no good at anything at all.

So, how do you train a neural network? There are basically two ways. One is through evolutionary algorithms, as I've described; the small changes to the program here refer to making small changes to the connection weights. I'll explain how evolution can be used to train neural networks to play games in the next section. The other important way of training a neural network is through making small changes in response to every time the network makes a mistake and sending these corrections backward in the neural network from the output layer to the input layer. This is called *backpropagation* and we'll see how that can be used in the section after next.

Survival of the Fastest

When I started my PhD back in 2004, my plan was to use evolutionary algorithms to train neural networks to control robots. These robots would be rewarded for doing such things as following other robots, not running into walls, solving a maze, and so on. Because neural networks that got more rewards would be able to procreate, in the end I would have a population of pretty well-behaving neural nets. That was the plan, at least. At that time, other researchers had already managed to teach robot-controlling neural networks to do these things, but I was going to do it ... better! I had a couple of ideas about connecting several neural networks together and training them one at a time, and such things. However, when I got down to the business of actually trying to teach neural nets to control these robots, I found out that this was a lot of hard work. The robots were slow and frequently put themselves in situations I would have to rescue them from, not to mention that I would have to contend with tires that wore down, cables that broke, and so on. It seemed to me that I was never going to make any real progress that way.

So I left the real world behind and turned to video games.

My idea was that I could use video games (instead of robots) as environments for testing my algorithms. Video games have most of the desirable qualities of a robotics problem and lack several of the highly undesirable qualities. In particular, you don't have to build an expensive robot or real-world obstacle course, you can speed up the game so your testing happens much faster (thousands of times faster in many cases) than real time, and when something goes wrong, you can just restart the game. You don't have to sweep up the pixels after your game character crashes, and you don't have to pay money to build a new one.

I decided to start with racing games because they have a nice difficulty curve: it's relatively straightforward to learn the very basics—just hit the accelerator to drive straight forward—but then things get more complicated when you also have to take curves and overtake other cars while avoiding colliding with them. And apparently there is a lot to learn about how to best conduct a car in a car race; otherwise, there would not be large recurring international competitions on this matter.[4] So I developed a simple car racing game and a way of driving cars with neural networks.

The way the neural network is used to drive the car is pretty simple: it connects the inputs of the neural network to what the driver "sees" and the outputs to the steering wheel and pedals. In one of my setups, I used eight neurons in the input layer: six were connected to simulated range-detecting sensors that returned the distance to the nearest track edge or other car each along six different directions, one to a speedometer, and one to a sensor that returned the angle relative to the track. The neural network had one hidden layer of six neurons, and finally the output layer had only two neurons, which were connected to the accelerator/brake and steering.

Take such a neural network with random connection weights and put it in control of a car, and it will either do nothing at all or do something rather uninteresting, like drive off the track and crash. Take a hundred such networks with different random connection weights, and some of them will do more interesting or useful things than the others. In order to turn this into an evolutionary algorithm, we need just a fitness function and a way of doing selection and mutation. In this case, the fitness function was very simple: how far the car drove in 30 seconds. Using a population of one hundred networks, the evolutionary algorithm I used would try all of the networks and remove the fifty networks that performed worst (drove the shortest distance in the time allotted); it would then replace them with copies of the fifty networks that performed best, but adding mutations in the form of randomly changing some of the connection weights in these networks.

This simple process worked like a charm. Within a dozen generations, I would have neural networks that could drive fairly well, and within one hundred generations I would typically get a neural network that could drive better than I could! Thus, I could yet again experience being beaten in a game by an AI program that I developed myself (an experience I highly recommend), but in contrast to that Checkers-playing program from my class assignment several years earlier, I had not really specified how the program should solve its task but rather how the program should learn to solve its task.

When I say the process worked like a charm, there's a hitch. It really did work like a charm when training the neural network to drive around a particular racetrack. When taking the same neural network and putting it in the car on a different racetrack, things did not work very well at all: mostly the car would fail to take turns when it should, and it veered off the track. I was a little confused by this, but then I realized that the track I had been training the neural networks to drive on was quite limited in the challenges it offered; for example, it contained only left turns. So I instituted a new training regime: every time the network learned how to drive well on one track, I added a new and different racetrack to the fitness function, so that the fitness of the neural network would depend on how it drove on several tracks. This approach worked very well, and relatively soon evolution produced neural networks that could drive proficiently on any track I could come up with for them, though in general they were a bit more careful drivers than the networks that had been evolved on a single track only.

Now what about racing in the presence of other cars? Not unsurprisingly, if you take a neural network that has been taught to drive on its own track undisturbed by pesky competitors and put it in a competitive race with other cars, mayhem ensues. Because the network has never encountered other cars before, it does not know how to avoid collisions, or that avoiding them is a good idea, or even what car-to-car collisions are. This can be rectified by training the network with other cars present and usually leads to pretty good driving behavior—depending on the fitness function. When we are no longer racing alone, we need to go back and think again about the fitness function.

The fitness function that works so well for learning to race alone on a track was to simply measure how far along the track the car travels in 30 seconds. But in a real competitive car race, what really matters is your position—ahead of or behind the other car(s)—so maybe the fitness function should reflect that. This would make the situation more like coevolution in the natural world, where the fitness of individuals in one species (or group, more generally) is partly dependent on another species— as with the example of rabbits and foxes earlier in this chapter. And it certainly seems that successful strategies in a car race, as in any other game, would be partly dependent on how other drivers drive.

To see what might happen if the fitness function mirrored the reward structure of an actual car race, I changed the fitness to a relative one—the position ahead of or behind the other car at the end of race. Very quickly, the evolutionary process found out that a viable strategy was to be very aggressive and push the other car off the track. This behavior seemed to be easier to learn than learning to drive fast, avoid collisions, and get a good lap time. Or perhaps a network that learned a nonaggressive strategy would be pushed out of the way by a neural network that learned an aggressive strategy, and therefore receive lower fitness. In any case, the composition of the fitness function could easily be used here as a knob to turn aggressiveness up or down in the evolved networks, something that could certainly be useful when creating interesting characters in games.

Trial and Error on Speed

Evolutionary computation can be described as a process of massive trial and error. It seems to be an enormously wasteful process—all those neural nets that are somewhat worse than the best neural nets of each generation are simply thrown away. None of the information they encountered in their brief "lives" is saved. Yet the process of evolution through selection works, both in nature (as we are living proof of) and inside computer programs. But is there another way we could learn from experience to create effective AI, perhaps preserving more information?

The problem of learning to perform a task given only intermittent feedback about how well you're doing is called the *reinforcement learning problem*, importing some terminology from behaviorist psychology (the kind where psychologists make rats pull levers and run around in mazes) to computer science. There are essentially two broad approaches to solving these problems. The less common is to use some form of evolutionary algorithm. The more common is to use some form of approximate dynamic programming, such as the *Q-learning* algorithm.

You can think of it this way: whereas evolutionary computing models the type of learning that takes place across multiple lifetimes, Q-learning (and similar algorithms) models the kind of learning that takes place during a lifetime. Instead of learning based on a single fitness value at the end of an attempt to perform a task (as evolution does), Q-learning can learn from many events as the task is performed. Instead of making random changes to the complete neural network (as happens in evolution), in Q-learning the changes are taken in specific directions in response to positive or negative rewards.

In Q-learning, the neural network takes inputs that represent what the agent "sees," just like the evolved car control network I described in the previous section. The networks also take inputs describing what action the agent is considering to take; in the car racing domain, it could be steer left, steer right, accelerate, and brake (or some combination). The output is a *Q-value*, which is an estimate of how good a particular action would be in a particular state (situation). So instead of mapping sensor inputs to actions, the network maps sensor inputs and actions to Q-values. The way this neural network is used to do something, such as driving a car, is that every time it needs to make a decision, it tests all possible actions and makes the one with the highest Q-value in the current state.

Obviously the neural network needs to be trained before it is useful; a network that outputs random Q-values is not going to win any races or solve any other problems, for that matter. The basic idea of training a neural network using Q-learning is to compare the predicted value of taking an action in a state with the actual value of taking the action in the state, as observed after having taken it. If the actual value differs from the predicted value, the neural network is adjusted a little bit using the back-propagation algorithm. For example, we don't know whether it's a good idea to turn left in an intersection. So we try it, and see what happens. Once we know what happens, we update our belief about the value of turning left in that intersection.

But how do we know the true value of taking a certain action in a given state? That depends on what feedback, or reinforcement, the agent gets from the world. For example, when teaching a neural network to car race, you may give it positive feedback (rewards) every time it reaches the goal or perhaps every time it clears a part of the track, and negative feedback (punishment) every time it veers off the track or bumps into another car. If the feedback is higher, or lower, than the network expected to get, then the backpropagation algorithm is used to slightly nudge the neural network in the direction of the feedback, so that it gives a better estimate of the value of that action the next time it encounters a similar state. The core of the Q-learning algorithm is to constantly update the neural network so that it becomes better at estimating how good a different action would be to take in a given state based on the rewards it gets now and then.

The problem with the procedure I just outlined is that you want to be able to tell how good actions are even when they are not rewarded right away. For example, if you are learning to drive a car, you want to learn that even going slightly off the racetrack is a bad idea, even though you would have to continue for several seconds before you actually exit the track and receive a negative reward (crash!). You also want to know that if you're at the starting line, accelerating is good even though it will take you quite some time until you actually complete the race and get a positive reward. Similarly, if you're playing *Tetris*, you want to know that stacking your blocks so that you can eventually clear several lines at the same time is a good idea, though it might be tempting to achieve short-term gains by clearing a single line. In real life, you might sometimes be in a state where a certain action, say ordering another drink, provides a short-term reward, but you may have learned that the action can have a negative value because of the long-term punishment of having a hangover the day after and increasing the risk of the longer-term punishment of ending up as an alcoholic. In reinforcement learning, this is called the *credit assignment problem*, and as you might expect, it's a very hard problem.

In Q-learning, the standard way of approaching the credit assignment problem is to learn from the *expected* reward. So every time an action is taken, if there's no actual reward or punishment from the world, it adjusts the neural network's estimate of the value of the action just taken based on its own estimate of the value of the best action in the next state. The neural network is essentially asking itself what it thinks its reinforcement should be. It sounds crazy, but given that the network now and then gets actual reinforcements from the world (or the game), this procedure should work—in theory. In practice, for a long time, it has been rather hard to get Q-learning to work reliably on complex problems. However, in 2015, a group of researchers at the London-based AI research company DeepMind managed to get Q-learning to play a number of classic arcade games from the Atari 2600 console, such as *Missile Command* and *Pac-Man*.[5] It took a lot of computer power to train these networks, more than a month of computer time per game, but the neural networks in many cases learned to play better than humans.

So which type of algorithm is better for learning to play games: Q-learning or evolution? In theory, Q-learning should be able to exploit more information because it can use more frequent reinforcement, and it can also make directed changes to the weights of the neural network, whereas evolution simply makes random changes. But it seems evolution has more freedom to invent strategies that are not directly dependent on the rewards, and evolution is also capable of changing the structure of the network, not just the weights. You could argue that Q-learning reacts to the feedback it gets by gradually tuning its strategies, whereas evolution boldly proposes complete new strategies and tests them as wholes.

In practice, both methods can work well when a skilled practitioner applies them. But we are still at the point when most learning methods don't work very well out of the box. In the long run, we could look at the natural world for inspiration: animals (including us) learn both during and across lifetimes, and it is likely that we would similarly need both types of learning to create systems that are able to learn really complex tasks by themselves.

6 Do Games Learn from You When You Play Them?

As we saw in the previous chapters, we learn from games—how to play them and almost certainly other skills as well. We can also develop algorithms that learn to play games. But let's turn this statement around. Can games learn from us? And if so, what could they learn? Can we develop algorithms that use our interactions with games to learn about us?

When you play a game, you are constantly supplying information to the game. You are pressing buttons and twiddling console sticks. In many games, you are also entering text. You are constantly making choices: go this way or that way, respond affirmatively or negatively to that character in a conversation, attack that enemy or not (and using which weapon). Some choices are complex and expressed over the course of a whole game, such as the personality and other characteristics of the character you are playing or the shape and political orientation of the country you rule; others happen at subsecond scales, such as exactly when to jump off a platform to avoid falling into a gap.

All of this is information that can be nicely expressed with numbers and other symbols. For games implemented on computers (including standard computer games as well as digital versions of board and card games), this is convenient because that's what computers are great at: storing and processing information. It's perfectly possible for a computer game to store all the input you have ever given it and then use clever algorithms to analyze it. These days, almost all devices we play games on (computers, smartphones, game consoles) are connected to the Internet. Given an Internet connection, it is perfectly possible for a game to "phone home" and send all the data it has gathered from you as you played it, either in raw form or aggregated, to the servers of the company that made the game. The game developer can then run all kinds of algorithms on the data to find out things about you and the rest of its player population. In fact, very many—maybe most?—recent video games already do this.

But what kinds of things can games learn from you?

What Would You Do?

Just like you can learn from a game how to play it, the game can learn from its players how it is played. By looking at the histories of how players have played the game, it is possible to find out what players typically do in each situation. This information can be used to create an AI that plays the game like an "average" player by simply taking the most frequent action in each situation. To see how this can be done, imagine that the game simply stores a long list of all the situations the player has ever been in (in the game) and the action the player took in each situation. Let's assume we can describe the situation with some numbers; for example, the coordinates of the player in the game world, current health, the relative position of the closest nonplayer characters (NPCs), and so on. After we've stored all these data in a long list, it becomes trivial to create an AI agent that can play the game just as the human player would. At every point in time, simply look at what situation the agent's character is in, find that situation in the long list of situations the player encountered, and take the action that the player took. Simple and elegant, right?

There are two problems with this simple solution. The first is that the list of all the situations a player has encountered can grow long—very long if you record where the player is, say, ten times per second and the player plays for ten hours, and very *very* long if you want to learn from not just one player but perhaps hundreds or millions. The length of the list is a problem not just for storing it in computer memory, but also for being able to look up one of these situations quickly. You don't want to look at millions of different stored actions every time you want to figure out what to do. We need a more compact way of storing the complete playing history of a player (or multiple players).

The other problem is that even if you spent ten hours playing a game, you have almost certainly not experienced every possible situation in that game. In fact, even if you have hundreds of players in your list, you are going to be missing lots of potential situations in your list. For every game that is not entirely trivial, the number of possible different game states is going to be some insanely large number, probably bigger than the number of stars in the universe.[1] You'll also need a way for your agent to deal with situations that the player(s) did not encounter. So we need a way to generalize.

Luckily, it turns out that you can use the backpropagation algorithm to train neural networks to predict what the player would do. Yes, this is the same method I described in the previous chapter when I talked about learning how to drive a car through trial and error. The difference is that here, we are using back-propagation not for reinforcement learning but for *supervised learning*. In supervised learning, you have a list of "instances," where each instance has a number of features that describe different aspects of the instance, and a target value. When learning to play the game like a human, each instance would be composed of the features describing a situation the player agent was in and what action the player took in the situation. Backpropagation is then used to train the neural network to reproduce this list. Remember that in reinforcement learning, the backpropagation algorithm changes the weights of the neural network depending on whether the action the network decided on leads to good or bad outcomes; in supervised learning, it changes the weights depending on whether the action the neural network decided on was the same as what the human decided on. Using this simple principle, the neural network can be trained to predict what action the player would have taken in each situation, usually with very good accuracy. The great advantage of this is that the neural network is much smaller than the long list of situations and actions used to train it, and it's much faster to "ask" the neural network for an action than it is to look up the state in a big table. Such neural networks typically also have a pretty good ability to generalize, meaning that they can come up with an answer for what the agent would do in a situation that the player never actually encountered based on what the player did in similar situations.

Who Are You in the Game?

For a game developer, it is crucial to know who plays their game: which aspects of it they are good and bad at, which aspects they like and dislike, and generally what they will do in the game. Outside the world of games, marketers use terms such as *target group analysis* and *market segmentation* when they talk about identifying and characterizing the potential customers of a product, so that the company that makes the product knows how to sell it or improve it. In games, we talk about player type analysis. The idea is that players of a game can be clustered into different groups, or player types, where the players of each type behave similarly and have similar preferences. An early and very influential attempt to identify player archetypes was made in the 1980s by Richard Bartle, a pioneer of online multiplayer games. Bartle built on his observations of players in the text-based online game *MUD* and stipulated four player types: *achievers*, who like to accumulate points and get ahead in the game; *explorers*, who like to explore both the space of the game and the rule system and find new places or invent new ways of playing; *socializers*, who are attracted to online games because of the opportunities to hang out with and talk to others; and finally, *killers*, who enjoy causing harm to other players' in-game characters.[2]

Obviously this typology works best for the type of games it was devised for: online multiplayer games. While the categories of achiever and explorer would be easy to apply to *Super Mario Bros.* and *Angry Birds* (and maybe Chess, though it is unclear what exploration means in such a game), the categories of socializer and killer make no sense for one- or two-player games. It is likely that you would need to find a different typology for each game or at least for each game genre. Fortunately, we have the tools to do this now, given all the data that games collect about us and modern data processing and machine learning techniques. In other words, games can learn player typologies from players.

In 2009, some of my colleagues at the IT University of Copenhagen (ITU), Alessandro Canossa, Anders Drachen, and Georgios Yannakakis, managed to get hold of a treasure trove of player data. Through a collaboration with the video game publisher Square Enix Europe, they gained access to data collected from about a million players playing *Tomb Raider: Underworld* on the XBox 360. The games in the *Tomb Raider* franchise are action-adventure games in which you play a single character (the adventurer Lara Croft) and navigate a three-dimensional world while solving puzzles and fighting bad guys and occasionally monsters (figure 6.1). The developers had included functionality in the code so that every time a player finished a level, the game contacted Square Enix's servers and uploaded a chunk of information about how the player had played the level. This information included how much time the player character had spent in various parts of the level, how many treasures found, how many enemies killed, and how often the player used the game's help system, among other things. This was a new and untested idea in 2009 (in 2018, it would be hard to find a commercially released game that does *not* "phone home" to the developer with information on how it's being played), and therefore the data were rather dirty and a lot of work was needed to get them into such shape that machine learning algorithms could be used on it.

The cleaned-up and reorganized data were fed to an algorithm known as a *self-organizing map*. This is a type of neural network. Like the ones discussed in the previous chapter, it is a computational structure inspired by the human brain, but it works rather differently from the car-driving networks discussed there. A self-organizing map takes a large amount of data and separates the instances into different groups so that the instances within one group are maximally similar and instances in different groups

Figure 6.1
Balancing on a ledge in *Tomb Raider: Underworld* (Crystal Dynamics, 2008).

are as different from each other as possible. In machine learning language, this is called *clustering* and is a form of *unsupervised learning* (as opposed to supervised learning or reinforcement learning). You don't know in advance how many groups you are going to get; this depends on the data and, to some extent, how you have configured the self-organizing map. In this case, each instance represented one player and contained carefully selected information about what sorts of things the player had done over the course of the game. Out came four clusters of data, representing four player types.

Simply knowing that there are four types of players doesn't tell us much. As a developer, we would want to know what those player types represent—in other words, how the players of one type differ from those of another. So the team looked at a number of representative players of each type and compared how much they had done each kind of action. They identified four types: *veterans*, who rarely die, collect most of the treasure, and generally play the game very well; *solvers*, who rarely use the help system or any hints, play slowly, and prefer to solve all of the game puzzles themselves; *runners*, who complete the game very quickly but frequently ask for help and tend to die more often; and *pacifists*, who are good at solving the game's puzzles but are bad at the combat elements and appear to seek to avoid them. This typology is clearly very different from Bartle's, which is understandable given that we are dealing with a very different type of game with a different player population. Something that is rather interesting is that the developers of the game at Square Enix had not foreseen the existence of the pacifist player type when they developed the game, and they were surprised to find out that the game was played in a way they had not "intended."[3]

While it is obviously useful to know what types of players play your game, it would perhaps be even more useful to know what the players are going to do in the game. Usually you want your players to stay with your game for as long as possible, because a happy player will recommend your game to a friend and perhaps buy your next game. It is also common with free-to-play games that are initially free but involve semi-mandatory payments for upgrades in order to keep playing. For developers of such games, it absolutely essential to be able to predict which players will stay with the game (and eventually pay money) and which might stop playing it. Why? Because when you know which aspects of your design make people stay and pay, you can tweak your game to make more money. In addition, as a game developer, you may simply be interested in understanding your players.

The next task for the same team, of which I was now a member (I had just moved to ITU to take up my first faculty position), as was Tobias Mahlmann (one of our PhD students), was to try to learn rules that would predict player behavior later in the game from player behavior early in the game. One of the things we tried to learn to predict was the highest level a player would complete out of the seven levels in the game. Theoretically, there are many supervised learning methods that could be used to learn to predict this, but some are better suited than others. We tried several of these methods on the task of predicting after which level the player would stop playing. One of the best-working methods was *decision tree induction*, a method that also has the advantage that its results are easy to understand for humans. It produces decision trees, which can be thought of as long lists of if-then rules within each other. Here is an example of what the algorithm learned:

```
IF Rewards on level 2 <18.5
THEN IF Time in Flushtunnel <9858: 2
ELSE (Time in Flushtunnel ≥9858): 3
ELSE (Rewards on level 2 ≥18.5): 7
```

In other words, if you accumulated a low score on level 2 and spent little time in the Flush Tunnel (an area in level 2), you will stop playing after level 2 and never finish level 3. Otherwise you will stop playing after level 3. However, if you accumulated a high score on level 2, you will finish the whole game.

This no doubt sounds like a very silly, arbitrary rule. It looks about as reasonable as astrology, and it's not the kind of rule you would expect an actual human game designer to come up with. However, silly as it may be, it is built on solid empirical evidence: it has a prediction accuracy of 76.7 percent when tested over tens of thousands of players. This means that while there are a certainly a few people who get a low reward on level 2 and then continue to finish the whole game, it is statistically unlikely. While it might be insulting to common sense that the amount of time spent in some tunnel should be so indicative of whether a player will give up the game after level 2 or 3, this really seems to be the case based on all these data. Maybe the most noteworthy result is that the prediction accuracy is so high. What this says is that we humans really are quite predictable, even when we play games.[4]

Who Are You Outside of the Game?

So far we have seen that the game can learn from your playing what type of player you are and how you will play in the future. But you are not only a player of games. You are a full-fledged human being, with hopes, dreams, fears, manners, friends, and habits. There is no reason to believe that all the rest of who you are disappears the moment you lean back on the sofa and grab the Xbox controller; you are still you, even if you are momentarily Mario, Master Chief, or Lara Croft. Now the question is, Does anything of the rest of you shine through in your game playing? What can the game learn about the real you from analyzing how you play?

Back in 2013, Alessandro and I had at our disposal an ambitious master's student, Josep Martinez, and we were searching for a topic for his thesis. Alessandro had recently read the works of Stephen Reiss, a personality psychologist who had devised a model for categorizing people's life motives, that is, what motivates them in life. Reiss identified sixteen broad life motives (in alphabetical order): acceptance, curiosity, eating, family, honor, idealism, independence, order, physical, power, romance, saving, social, status, tranquility, and vengeance. Each of these motives has several subcategories, and there is a well-tested questionnaire available for assessing life motives. We wondered whether the motives people had in real life were also expressed in games. If so, which ones? And in which games?

Like so many others, Alessandro, Josep, and I were fascinated by *Minecraft*, the open world game that took the world by storm beginning in 2010. When it was first released, as a buggy beta, *Minecraft* was a rather unique game—now there are many clones—not only for its peculiarly blocky graphics but also for the unparalleled freedom it affords players. The game is now a global phenomenon that is used for everything from making machinima (animated films made inside video games), to education, to testing AI algorithms. *Minecraft* can be described as a cross between a role-playing game and a digital version of Lego (figure 6.2). When you arrive in the game, you have nothing, and you must hurry to assemble some tools so you can build yourself some shelter before the night comes and monsters start roaming the land. But in order to make these tools, you need materials, and in order to get those, you need to mine the ground. After crafting more advanced tools, you will be able to mine deeper for more exotic materials so you can construct more advanced buildings and mechanisms. Given enough time and effort, you can construct anything you want. Searching for videos of *Minecraft* on YouTube yields thousands of examples of player-constructed replicas of famous buildings and vehicles (even the *Starship Enterprise*). There is also a storyline in *Minecraft*, including fairly typical role-playing game-like quests, but it is entirely optional whether to follow this storyline and carry out the quests; many players don't.

Figure 6.2
The cubistic world of *Minecraft* (Mojang, 2011). The game largely revolves around mining cubes for material so that you can build things
out of other cubes.

Almost all games afford a number of different playing styles,
but *Minecraft* does so more than most others. I think it's safe to
say that there are more different ways to play *Minecraft* than there
are ways to play *Tomb Raider: Underworld*. Clearly these different
playing styles reflect different in-game motivations: some people
are motivated by finishing quests, others by expressing themselves through building grandiose edifices, yet others by collecting rare resources. But do these motivations have anything to
do with your real-world life motives? Does someone who cares
mostly about her family play differently from someone whose

chief concern is getting ahead in professional life? We decided to find out.

Josep sent out questionnaires, with questions taken from the Reiss Motivation Profile, to 100 *Minecraft* players; these questionnaires were used to construct a profile of each player in terms of what motivated them most. He then asked each player for her *Minecraft* log file. This is a small file automatically saved by the game, which contains more than six hundred variables, including such things as how many hours the player has played, how much redstone ore she has mined (redstone is used for making electric-like circuits), and how far she has traveled by pig (an often overlooked transportation option). After extracting and cleaning these data, we ran a correlation analysis of all combinations of potentially relevant game variables and life motives.

"Correlation" is a way of saying that, statistically, two things have something to do with each other. It does not necessarily mean that one causes the other: if umbrella sales and the number of hours you spend watching TV are correlated across the weeks in a year, they might both be caused (at least in part) by bad weather. Two variables can correlate negatively or positively. So is, for example, smoking negatively correlated to longevity: when one is high, the other is low. (In this case, it is reasonable to assume that one causes the other.)

We found that all of the life motives were significantly correlated with several of the in-game variables. However, some were correlated with only a few variables (so few that it might come down to chance), whereas others were correlated with a large number of the in-game variables, and some of the correlations were so strong that there was virtually no room for doubt. Among the most highly correlated life motives were curiosity, saving, vengeance, and honor, whereas those that did not seem to be much expressed in the game were romance, tranquility, and physical activity. In some cases, these correlations make intuitive sense to someone who knows the game; in other cases, they are unexpected and quite amusing. People who are strongly motivated by curiosity in real life tend to craft plenty of torches and stone tools in the game, which makes sense because these are the most cost-efficient ways of exploring large parts of the game world. Those who are motivated by saving tend to use cheap and simple materials in the buildings and tools they construct. Vengeful players apparently quit the game and restart it (perhaps from an earlier save) more often—what would be called "rage quit" in gamer lingo. Players who are strongly motivated by independence in real life showed this in the game by refusing to do the quests in the game's storyline; in particular, it was strongly correlated with not even attempting the final quest. Another interesting expression of life motives is that people with a strong need for tranquility built significantly more fences around their dwellings. It certainly seems that the person you play when you play *Minecraft* is you in some very important respects.[5]

These results can be seen in the light of the studies by Nick Yee, then at Stanford University, and his colleagues, who investigated how players express their personality (rather than life motives) in the online multiplayer role-playing game *World of Warcraft* (figure 6.3). Yee used the Big Five personality questionnaire, which groups personality traits into the five categories of Openness, Conscientiousness, Extraversion, Agreeableness, and Neuroticism. There were plenty of correlations in these data as well, and he could see, for example, that conscientious players were more likely to collect items of various kinds and less likely

Figure 6.3
World of Warcraft (Blizzard, 2004) is a massively multiplayer online role-playing game; much of the game is communicating with other players over text or voice chat.

to die of accidents, that players with high openness explored more of the game world, and that extraverted players (unsurprisingly) had more social interactions in the game.[6] A group led by Pieter Spronck and including Shoshanna Tekofsky at the University of Tilburg has also found similar effects in games as different as the epic strategy game *Civilization* and the first-person shooter *Battlefield 4*. For example, it's possible to predict gender and age with relatively good accuracy from how people play *Battlefield 4*.[7]

Taken together, the picture we get from this research, as well as many other studies on these topics, is that you express quite a lot of yourself while playing games. If the game wants to, it can find out not only who you are in-game and how you will play in the future, but also quite a lot about who you are outside of the game. This raises plenty of interesting opportunities not only for game developers but also for psychologists and other social scientists who want to understand how humans function.

But this research also raises a number of complicated questions. A couple of years ago, I was speaking at a conference where a number of people from the security services and other government agencies were in attendance. One of the things I talked about was how much you could find out about players from their in-game behavior. In order to stir the conversation, I suggested that it might be possible to find out really sensitive information about players, such as their political views, sexuality, history of drug use and incarceration, or health status. (Note: I have not done this research and do not intend to!) I was expecting to get some worried reactions, but instead these people simply nodded pensively, as in "that's an interesting idea." It is fair to say that I have not become less worried about the potential to use player modeling for nefarious purposes since then. Particularly in light of concerns about how much of our personal information is gathered by security services, social network companies, internet providers, and all manners of shady operators who sell their services to the highest bidder, I think it is important to realize that our game playing is another way in which we leave rich digital trails. The difference, perhaps, is that when we post on a social network, we are aware that we are sharing information about ourselves; when we play a game, this is not obvious because we believe we are only acting inside the game world. But as we have seen, we bring much of ourselves into that world.

7   Automating Creativity

Ada Lovelace is widely considered the world's first programmer. She was the first to write programs for Charles Babbage's *Analytic Engine*, a very ambitious but never realized mechanical computer, in the mid-nineteenth century. She was also among the first to point out the truly marvelous potential of computing machines. In her view, however, the "Analytical Engine has no pretentions whatsoever to *originate* anything. It can do *whatever we know how to order it to perform.*" In the last century and a half we have seen massive progress in computing, in particular since the invention of the actual digital computers. However, surprisingly many would still believe something like the following: *Although we can make computers play games, predict what players will do, and even associate certain player behaviors with personality characteristics, the computers could never design the games themselves. For that, we need human creativity because computers can never fundamentally create something that we humans didn't program them to do first.*

This is entirely wrong and one of the most harmful widespread myths about computing and artificial intelligence. While "automating creativity" might sound like an oxymoron to some, creativity is in fact no more or less automatable than other human cognitive capabilities. In this chapter, I discuss some ways in which artificial intelligence methods can be used to do things that would be called "creative" if humans did them, in particular when it comes to designing games. I will also look at how we could use artificial intelligence to augment our own creativity for such design tasks. But first, let's rewind the tape a decade.

In 2006, I was two years into my PhD, and I had published several papers on ways of evolving neural networks to drive cars or play other games. These papers had been well received by the research community, but they were not groundbreaking. I had shown that neuroevolution could work well for this type of game, but in the end, what I had done was just to take a well-known method in robotics and shown how to make it work for certain types of games. I was wondering what the next step in my doctoral project would be. One idea I was toying with was to try to use more complex information, such as raw visual data, as input to the neural network, but this didn't seem exciting enough.

But then one day, while I was thinking in the shower, I had another idea. Evolutionary algorithms are apparently very useful for creating agents (implemented as neural networks) that can play a game. But could you use the same principle, evolution, to create other parts of the game—for example, the levels?[1]

I mentioned this idea to my friend Renzo De Nardi, who found it interesting and agreed to help out. Because there was a suitable conference and its deadline was just over a week away, we figured that we should have enough time to refine the concept, write the code, design and run the experiment, and write the paper. (Unfounded optimism and willingness to work all through the night are useful assets when doing a PhD.) We chose the same racing game I had built for my previous experiments in evolving neural nets to drive cars because we already knew how that code worked. We immediately faced two problems: how to represent the racing tracks so that evolution can search for good tracks effectively and how to create a fitness function that accurately tells us how "good," or enjoyable, a racing track is.

The first problem is not exactly trivial but not that hard to solve, either. We represented the tracks using a technique called *b-splines*, where a track can be described by a sequence of numbers specifying how the track bends. So just as for neural networks, the "genome" of a racing track is simply a list of numbers.

The second problem is much trickier and immediately brings up fundamental problems in aesthetics. How do we know that a racetrack, or some other type of game level, or any type of game content, is any good? If we try to be a little more specific, how can we write program code that automatically evaluates a racetrack and returns a number corresponding to how exciting, or interesting, or entertaining a human would think that racetrack is when playing a racing game? On the face of it, this seems like an impossible task. How could we know what a human would think of a game level without having that human around? We would have to simulate the whole human and ask the simulation what it thinks—something that, mildly put, is well beyond our technical capabilities. If you are still not convinced about how hard this is, imagine writing a program that would look at paintings and given them a score between 1 and 10 reflecting how much a professional art critic would like the painting. It's hard to even imagine where to begin. Problems like these are sometimes called *AI-complete problems*, reflecting the idea that you first need to develop general human-level AI to be able to solve them.

However, as with many other very hard problems, it turns out you can make a good deal of progress if you don't care about getting things exactly right, and instead just try to get some rough approximation. In our case, we looked into game design theory[2] and also played a couple of racing games ourselves to see if we could discover some simple rules that would indicate that indicate that one racetrack was better than another. We came up with the following heuristic rules for what makes a good racetrack:

- It should have the right difficulty.
- It should have different types of challenges along a lap, such as some sharp turns and some smooth curves.
- At some point on the track, it should be possible to drive really fast.

How can we measure whether a track has these properties? Well, the simplest way is to drive the track and see what happens. We could look at whether the driver manages to complete the lap, the difference in minimum and maximum speed along the track (indicating that there are different types of challenges), and the maximum speed achieved. We can then create a fitness function that reflects all three of these values, allowing the evolutionary algorithm to search for tracks with all three of the properties we listed.

The remaining problem, then, is that someone will need to drive the car. We can't have an actual human do the driving because the evolutionary algorithm will need to try thousands or even tens of thousands of different tracks with minor variations, and humans are far too slow for that and also get tired easily. We needed an artificial player to drive our tracks in order to evaluate their quality. Luckily, I had been working on evolving neural networks for driving cars in this particular racing game, so we could use those neural network drivers to test the tracks. Even better, we could train neural networks to drive like us, so we could evolve racetracks that would suit our own driving styles, using a combination of evolutionary algorithms and the backpropagation method I described in the previous chapter.

Renzo and I trained some neural networks to drive like us. Appropriately, the network trained on data from my playthroughs drove fast and recklessly, while the network trained on Renzo's playthroughs drove slowly and meticulously. (Note that this only reflects our driving styles in racing games; in offline life, I don't actually have a driver's license.) We then evolved racing tracks to fit each of our driving styles. The results are in figure 7.1.

I've since worked with various teams of people to take this general idea—creating new game levels with evolution, using agents that play the levels to evaluate them—to various games and level types. For example, we showed that we could automatically create

Figure 7.1
The racetracks that evolved from the neural networks.

balanced maps for *StarCraft* and levels for *Super Mario Bros*. We call the general idea "search-based procedural content generation," because game content is generated through a search process—in this case, based on artificial evolution. All that is needed is a good way of representing the game content and a good fitness function (though, as we've seen, this part can be tricky).[3]

The idea of seeing creativity as a search in a space of potential artifacts is not new; it has been discussed at length by, for example, the British philosopher Margaret Boden.[4] There are also many examples of search-based approaches to generating music, images, and so on. Seeing creativity as search, it becomes clear that creativity is about as automatable as any other endeavor that usually requires human thought: it's by no means easy but definitely not impossible.

The Random Number God

The idea of creating some parts of games automatically, through algorithms, is not new, either. In fact, it is almost as old as video games themselves. Back in the days when computing power was a scarce resource available only on mainframe computers you had to share with hundreds or thousands of others, and even that mainframe had far lower processing speed and far less storage capacity than a cell phone has today, conserving bytes was of the utmost importance. This was the environment in which Michael Toy and Glenn Wichmann created *Rogue* in 1980 (figure 7.2).

Toy and Wichmann, who were studying at the University of California at Santa Cruz, were aficionados of the influential pen-and-paper role-playing game *Dungeons and Dragons*. Normally, *Dungeons and Dragons* campaigns require a specialized dungeon master who runs the game and plays various NPC roles in the game world where a team of one or several players is adventuring. Toy and Wichmann wondered how they could create a computer game that played a bit like *Dungeons and Dragons* but could be played alone, against the computer. Translating the combat mechanics from *Dungeons and Dragons* into code was easy enough. The problem was with the adventures, which, in *Dungeons and Dragons*, appropriately enough often take place in dungeons. In *Dungeons and Dragons*, these dungeons are either made by the dungeon master or bought in books sold by the game publisher. Clearing a dungeon involves navigating a maze to find the exit; collecting items; managing health, food, and money; and fighting (and/or running away from) monsters. For the game the duo was creating, *Rogue*, they didn't want to create the dungeons themselves because they created the game primarily for themselves and it would be more fun to be surprised by the dungeons. In any case, they simply didn't have the disk space to store many dungeons for the game, so handcrafting them was practically impossible.

Necessity is supposedly the mother of invention, so Toy and Wichmann were forced to invent a way of automatically generating dungeons. Every time a new game of *Rogue* is started, a completely new dungeon is created, and this procedure was fast even back on 1980-era computers. The algorithm, somewhat simplified here, works as follows. First, divide the dungeon into different segments; then create rooms in all the dungeon segments; mark the first one that is visited; then keep creating corridors from (randomly chosen) visited rooms to (randomly chosen) unvisited rooms until all rooms are marked as visited. This will create a number of rooms that are connected by corridors, so that it is possible to get from any room to any other.

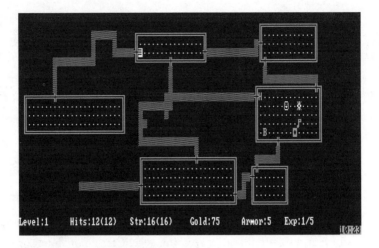

Figure 7.2
Rogue (A. I. Design, 1980), the original roguelike, has modest hardware requirements because it was developed for a computer that had less computational power than your fridge. The smiley face represents the player character.

What's left is to add items and monsters; these are mostly sprinkled out at random in the rooms.

The result of this process is that every game of *Rogue* feels fresh. Every time you start playing the game, there's a new dungeon for you to find your way in, new potions to figure out, new monsters to kill. This means that to become good at playing the game, you need to learn strategies for how to play the game well rather than simply memorize the layout of the dungeons. This is a qualitatively different kind of game play compared to many other types of games.

While *Rogue* was not the first game to include procedurally generated levels (that distinction may belong to the slightly earlier and simpler *Beneath Apple Manor*), its popularity led to the

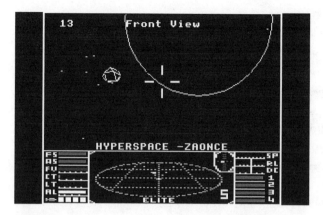

Figure 7.3
Approaching a space station in *Elite* (Acornsoft, 1984).

creation of a new genre of games called "roguelikes" in honor of the landmark game. By definition, every roguelike game session presents a new set of levels to play. Many are also role-playing games like *Rogue*, for example, the open source classic *NetHack*, the endlessly intricate *Dwarf Fortress*, or Blizzard's best-selling *Diablo* series. But many other games that are not commonly thought of as roguelikes build on the idea of generating levels, or worlds at the start of every playing session. This includes some very well-known games; the indie sensation platformer *Spelunky*, the epic strategy games in the *Civilization* series, or the mega-selling sandbox game *Minecraft* (also discussed in the previous chapter); none of these games would be possible in anything like their current format without procedural generation.

Another game from the 1980s that spearheaded procedural content generation is *Elite* (figure 7.3), a space trading and battle game where the player explores a galaxy with thousands of planets, buys and sells goods and items, fights space pirates, and takes on missions. The scale of the game is large by any standard, but what is even more impressive is the extremely limited hardware it ran on. I played it on my Commodore 64, a popular home computer with 64 kilobytes of memory. How could such a huge game world possibly fit into 65,536 characters' worth of memory, especially given that the game engine and graphics needed to be stored there as well? The answer is that every star system was generated as you visited it, including names and positions of planets and space stations, prices of commodities, and locations of spaceships. But unlike *Rogue*, the game does not change with every play session, and if you go back to a star system you've left, you'll find it looks just as the way it did when you left it. This is because *Elite* uses a particular *seed* value for the random number generator for each star system, precisely determining the output of the generative algorithm. Instead of storing thousands of star systems, *Elite* simply stores the number of each star system and uses that to regenerate the star system as it needs. This idea has been highly influential in game development and is used in various roles in many games for regenerating things such as vegetation on demand. A prominent recent example of a game storing a complete galaxy as seed values, creating a giant space for the player to explore, is *No Man's Sky* (figure 7.4).

So does this mean that the problem of procedural content generation is already solved? Far from it. The problem can be illustrated by the Random Number God. When starting a game of *Rogue*, most of the time you'll get a dungeon of reasonable difficulty, but sometimes you can get crazy difficulty spikes or long sequences with little challenge. Also, some dungeons are just (much) better than others. So it has become common to blame an unfair outcome in *Rogue* (or another roguelike) on the Random Number God, who clearly was out to get the player by

Figure 7.4
In *No Man's Sky* (Hello Games, 2016) all planets are procedurally generated, including their flora, fauna, and geology.

spawning his character right next to a high-level dragon, or in a room that is almost impossible to get out of, or something else like that.

The problem is that it is very hard to foolproof the type of algorithms used by games such as *Rogue*. In other words, it is hard to make sure that the level that comes out at the other end is always at the right level of difficulty, or balanced, or sometimes even playable. This, of course, limits what kind of games we can procedurally generate levels for using these methods. Here is where the search-based approach shines. With a well-designed fitness function based on an agent playing the level, it becomes possible to include as a condition that the level is indeed balanced, playable and having the right level of challenge. This makes procedural generation of game content possible in a much wider range of games, bringing us closer to the vision I outlined in chapter 4.

Getting Personal

The vision I laid out in chapter 4 also includes that the game somehow adapts to you and creates new content that is not just good in general but tailored specifically to you: what you like, what you're good at, and how you play. Using search-based procedural content generation, we can create levels that can be played by an artificial agent trained on a particular player's playing style, so we can at least indirectly adapt the new levels to the skills and playing style of a human player. But how could we create levels that are adapted to the *preferences* of a human, levels that would be tailored to create a particular kind of experience in the player?[5]

This was the question that my friend and colleague Georgios Yannakakis and I asked ourselves in 2009. Georgios had been working on methods for modeling player experience for his PhD thesis and several years after that. He had developed machine learning–based methods for predicting what a player would think of a particular part of a game. I had been working on the search-based approach to procedural content generation, as described above. We thought that there should be some way of combining these two ideas to automatically generate game content that would create a specific experience in the player.

We recruited a master's student, Chris Pedersen, for the project and started collecting data. Because we needed lots of data, we wanted to use a game that many already knew, so we were delighted to find *Infinite Mario*, an open-source clone of Nintendo's classic platformer *Super Mario Bros*. We modified the level generator so that it could create levels according to parameters (figure 7.5). These parameters specified properties such as how large the holes in the ground should be and how far from each

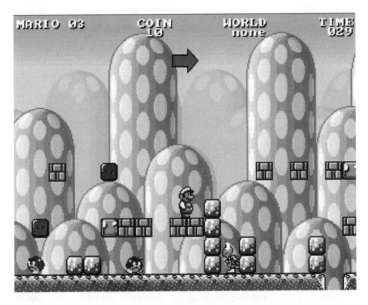

Figure 7.5
Part of a level generated in the *Mario* AI framework using an evolutionary algorithm.

other enemies should appear. By varying these parameters, we could get the generator to generate very different kinds of levels, some largely empty, some with lots of enemies to defeat, others with tricky jumping challenges, and so on. We created a few hundred levels with very different settings of these parameters and proceeded to try to get people to play games for us.

While most people enjoy playing games, getting hundreds of people to play your game so you can collect data about them is not easy at all. Sometimes you have to pay people to play games. For this experiment, however, it was enough to pester our friends using Twitter, Facebook, and email (no one has so far unfriended me over this kind of behavior—as far as I know). Each person was tasked with playing at least two levels of the game. Those two levels were generated using different parameter values so that they felt different to play. Each person played different pairs of levels. We recorded everything the player did while playing, and after each pair of levels, we asked them a set of questions, Which of the two levels just played was more challenging? Which was more entertaining? Which was more frustrating?

After collecting data from more than seven hundred players, we set out to try to create a model of player experience. We defined a neural network (figure 7.6) that would take the parameters of two different levels as inputs, along with some data on the player's playing style, such as how often the player jumped, how much the player ran, and how many enemies the player defeated. The three outputs of the neural network represented the player's preference: which of the two levels they found more challenging, more entertaining, and more frustrating. Once we had the data, training the neural network to accurately predict player preferences was straightforward. We now had a model of player preference that, given two levels in the game and a particular playing style, could predict which of the two levels the player would prefer in each of these three dimensions.

The next step was to use this model to generate new levels. For this part of the project, we brought on our promising new PhD student, Noor Shaker, who got to work on building what we called an *experience-driven* procedural content generator. It turned out to be easier than expected: given that the neural network we trained can predict which levels a particular person would prefer, we can use it as a fitness function. You simply evolve the level parameters to maximize how much the neural

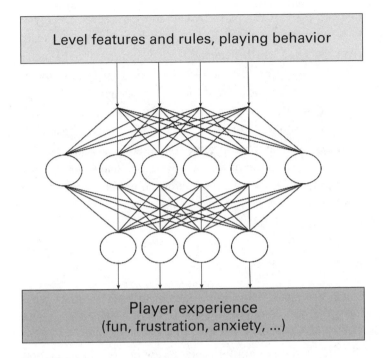

Figure 7.6
Diagram of a neural network that takes level design parameters and play-ing style as inputs, and outputs predicted player affect. By keeping play-ing style constant and optimizing for desired player affect, we can find out what types of levels would likely cause certain experiences in the player.

network predicts the player would enjoy the level. Once you have these level parameters, you feed them into the standard level generator, which generates levels that turn out to be pretty exactly what you asked for. (As usual, this description ignores a number of technical details and tricky design decisions, but conceptually this is what happens.) A nice feature of this procedure is that you can optimize for each of the three dimensions of preference separately or in some combination. So, for example, you can search for levels that would be maximally entertaining and minimally frustrating for a particular player. Of course, you can also search for levels that are minimally entertaining and maximally frustrating (if that's what you prefer).

Getting More General

So far, I've talked about game content in a very abstract sense but given only examples of game levels (if we count racetracks and dungeons as levels). What other things could we generate? Well, it's very common for games to use procedural generation of vegetation such as trees and grass and other natural features such as clouds and water. Generating such "background" content is pretty much a solved problem, and there is software that will take care of it for you if you want. The reason things such as bushes and clouds are simple to generate is that they don't need to interact too much with the rest of the game and its mechanics. An oddly shaped cloud or bizarre tree might raise a few eyebrows but will not make your game unplayable. But what if we look in the other direction, at generating content that is core to the game and interacts with everything? Could we generate game rules? Maybe even complete games?

In 2008, Cameron Browne was finishing his PhD thesis on exactly this topic. He'd done his PhD mostly on weekends and evenings while working as a software developer and also indulging in his other hobby: designing board games and writing books about designing board games. (I know him and can confirm that he sometimes sleeps as well.) For his PhD, he had designed the *Ludi* language and game generation system, specifically focused on so-called *recombination games*: games with regular boards and pieces of only a few types, like Checkers, Go, Hex, and Othello.[6] The Ludi language allows such games to be represented in only a few lines of code, where one line defines the board size and shape, another line defines how and if pieces can be captured, and so on. This code can be treated as a genome, so game rules can be created with an evolutionary algorithm. To get the evolutionary algorithm going, Cameron supplied the Ludi system with dozens of existing recombination games, mostly classic games, to serve as the initial population. He also designed a fitness function that would evaluate the quality of the games through playing them and measuring a number of properties of the playthrough, such as how often the lead changed and how early in the game it was possible to predict who would win (it's generally considered a good thing if you can predict this as late as possible). With the representation and fitness function specified, Ludi could start evolving games. This was of course a very slow process because the system needed to play every game it came up with many times against itself. But the results were worth the wait. In particular, one game, *Yavalath* (figure 7.7), was so novel and good that a game publisher was interested in selling the game as a boxed set in stores. This is probably the world's first completely computer-generated commercial game.

Figure 7.7
Yavalath (Nestorgames, 2007) was designed by the Ludi system, which was designed by Cameron Browne.

As far as I'm aware, however, Cameron gets all the royalties from the game sales, with none of the money going to Ludi.

At the same time that Cameron was working on Ludi, I was working on my own ideas for generating game rules. But unlike Cameron, whose system works on a specific kind of board game, I was targeting simple arcade games in the style of *Pac-Man*. I took axioms that these games would take place in two-dimensional game worlds and that the player controlled an agent that could move around and interact with various "things." The way I thought about this was that the various things could be enemies, food, bonuses, friends, mines, or something else, all depending on how they interacted with each other and with the player. For example, in *Pac-Man*, pellets disappear when interacting with the player agent and increase score, and the player-agent disappears if interacting with a ghost. So I decided to evolve the rules for how these things interacted. When designing the fitness function, I was inspired by Raph Koster's idea that fun in games comes from learning, as detailed in chapter 2. I wanted to evolve learnable games, but of course I couldn't use actual humans in the fitness function. Instead, I used another evolutionary algorithm—inside the fitness function, inside the main evolutionary algorithm—that would try to learn to play the game. Games where the algorithm could make quick improvements got high fitness scores.[7]

Alas, my experiments did not result in any new hit games to rule the App Store. What I got was a number of examples of games that the fitness function thought were reasonable but for various reasons were not interesting to play, or sometimes weren't even playable. It turns out that generating video game rules is significantly harder than generating rules for board games such as recombination games. One reason is that for the fitness function to work well, we need an AI agent that is able to not only play any strange game that the evolutionary algorithm throws at it but also play them well and in a human-like manner. Note that if you are part of a fitness function, you are bound to encounter some very strange games produced by random mutations and crossover. This is very much an unsolved research problem.

Together with various students and collaborators, I've kept up the efforts to develop algorithms that can create rules for video games. In one project, we used the Video Game Description Language (discussed in chapter 9) as representation and tried to evolve games that good agents do well at and bad agents do

Figure 7.8
To That Sect (Michael Cook, 2014) was designed by the ANGELINA system, which was designed by Michael Cook.

poorly at—in other words, games that have some *skill depth*. This has had some limited success, being able to create novel rules for simple puzzle games in the style of *Sokoban*.[8] Others have also been working on this, for example Adam Smith has proposed using logic programming to create game rules,[9] and Mike Cook has worked for a long time on ANGELINA, a multifaceted system that can generate not only rules but all kinds of different game assets, with fascinating results (figure 7.8).[10]

Trying to create systems that can create games is not only about building technical systems that can do marvelous things. Since its inception, artificial intelligence has had the dual purpose of creating systems that can solve tasks that seem to require intelligence and to understand the principles behind the intelligence that already exists in the world, for example, in us. More generally, one of the things you learn as a computer scientist is that you don't really understand a task until you have written program code that can solve that task. This is because only designing and implementing an algorithm that solves a task forces you to look at the task in sufficient detail. This is true even of such a mundane thing as sorting: studying and implementing sorting algorithms forces you to understand sorting in depth. I am sure you intuitively know how to sort socks or pencils or coins, but unless you have taken computer science classes, you have probably not thought much about exactly which rules you follow when you sort things, and how sorting could be made more efficient. This observation is even more true for game design, a complex endeavor that we can (imperfectly) train people to do but that we don't understand at anything like the depth with which we understanding tasks such as sorting, text reading, or car driving. Designing and implementing systems that can perform some aspect of game design, even if in a very limited environment, is therefore a way of studying game design.

Being Creative Together

For the foreseeable future, we will not have AI systems that can design a complete game from scratch with anything like the quality, or at least consistency of quality, that a team of human game developers can. Human designers will not be out of a job anytime soon. However, there are a number of problems for which AI methods already perform impressively, as we have seen. In many cases, the strengths of human designers and algorithms are complementary rather than replacing each other. This suggests that we could build systems where humans collaborate with AI algorithms to make games—for example, by using algorithms for ideation, feedback, fine-tuning, and automatic play testing. In particular, this could be done through building *mixed-initiative* AI-assisted game design tools. These are systems in which both the human user and the AI can take initiatives when it comes to editing the game and where the AI can provide suggestions, feedback, and limited automated generation for the human user.

One influential example of such a system is Tanagra by Gillian Smith, now a professor at Worcester Polytechnic Institute.[11] Tanagra is an editor for platform games that uses constraint solving to generate whole levels or parts of levels. The user can create levels completely freely, but at any time can call on the tool to generate a completely new level or just regenerate any particular part of a level. The level generator ensures that every level is playable.

Inspired by this system, Antonios Liapis, at the time a PhD student of Georgios Yannakakis and myself, started working on a system we call Sentient Sketchbook.[12] The idea was to unify several different types of AI-based design support in a system that would help create levels for strategy games. In Sentient Sketchbook, the user works on "map sketches," somewhat abstract representations of strategy game maps (see figure 7.9). As the user edits the map, the tool provides feedback about such measures as how balanced the map is, how close resources are to base locations, and how protected bases are. Some of these quantities are visualized as gauges and some as overlays on the actual map, for example, displaying graphically which resources are under the control of a particular base location. The tool also constantly provides users with suggestions for ways of improving the map. These suggestions are generated by evolutionary algorithms running in the background, at every point in time starting from the current map design and asking questions like these: What

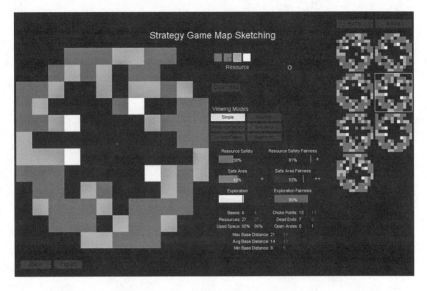

Figure 7.9
Editing a map sketch with Sentient Sketchbook.

would it be like if the map was a little more balanced, or had fewer impassable areas, or maybe resources that were harder to control? The user is of course free to disregard any suggestions; Sentient Sketchbook will keep trying to second-guess the designer's intent.

Tools like Tanagra and Sentient Sketchbook—and several others that have followed in their footsteps—show the way toward greater use of AI methods in game design and development.[13] A combination of algorithms and human designers is in almost any case better than either on their own. I predict we will soon see similar tools integrated into mainstream game engines such as Unity and Unreal.

But will we also see modern AI methods applied within games, as opposed to for design and development, anytime soon?

8   Designing for AI

In chapter 4, I posed the question why the type of artificial intelligence methods we have seen so many examples of in this book are not used more in games. I outlined a couple of potential reasons for this. One of the reasons I mentioned is that game development is a surprisingly risk-averse industry because of the hit-driven nature of the business and that the technology may not be mature enough yet. Now, after spending the past few chapters on AI methods for playing games, modeling players, and generating content, we'll revisit the question. This time we focus on the role of game design in enabling AI and, conversely, AI in enabling game design.

Back when I was a naive and overenthusiastic PhD student, and even when I was a slightly less naive and overenthusiastic postdoc, I tried rather naively to effect change. When I met a game designer or developer at a conference, I would try to convince her that her company's new game stood to win a whole lot by using some of these fancy new AI methods. Usually the response I would get was that no, in fact their game did not need my AI at all; it works perfectly fine as it is. For example, while we could train a neural network to drive a car faster or provide a more challenging opponent in a fighting game, this is unnecessary because it's easier to simply artificially manipulate the top speed of computer-controlled cars or hit boxes of nonplayer character (NPC) fighters until they get the desired performance. Basically, why introduce complex AI when you could simply cheat? And, anyway, the game would get boring if the enemies were too hard because the fun comes from beating them. It's true that we could use online adaptation, maybe through reinforcement learning, to create a game character that learns from your behavior in a role-playing game and updates its own behavior to match what you do; but this runs the very real risk of ruining the carefully tuned game balance and making the game unplayable. Sure, we could build a level generation algorithm that enables an endless supply of new competitive multiplayer levels for a first-person shooter; but the game already has a couple of good levels and most players prefer to play the levels they already know.

I found this attitude extremely conservative and annoying, but after a while, I had to admit that in many cases, they were right. Many games would not actually benefit from advanced AI because they were designed to not need any AI.

Let me explain. Most of today's video game genres have their roots in games developed in the 1980s and early 1990s. These eras saw the development of platformers, role-playing games, puzzle games, turn-based and real-time strategy games, team sports games, first-person and third-person shooters, construction and management simulations, racing games, and so on. While there has certainly been design innovation since 2000—for example, the invention of multiplayer online battle arenas (MOBAs) such as *League of Legends* and sandbox games such as *Minecraft*—these new game genres evolved from earlier genres.

Back in the 1980s and early 1990s, artificial intelligence was much less advanced than it is today. While the fundamental algorithm behind modern deep learning, backpropagation, had been invented, it was far less understood than it is today, and many of the inventions that make neural networks work so well had not been made yet. Monte Carlo tree search did not exist, and although evolutionary algorithms were an active field of research, major advances have been made since. Most important, though, was that computer power was very limited then. Depending on what you measure, your current laptop is at least tens of thousands of times as fast as the computers that genre-defining games such as *DOOM* and *Dune 2* were designed to run on, and your smartphone is faster than the fastest supercomputers of the 1980s. On top of that, the ability to run neural networks on graphics cards (GPUs) did not exist back then; its invention has added another few orders of magnitude of speed for deep learning in particular.

When the games that came to define whole genres were developed, incorporating state-of-the-art artificial intelligence was not an option. I don't think that a design goal for early platformers was to have (only) enemies that moved back and forth in predictable patterns. It also seems improbable that it was considered a good thing in early role-playing games that the NPCs say the same canned lines all the time and force you to navigate cumbersome dialogue trees and, presumably, the level generation in early roguelikes was not meant to be highly erratic and disregard the player's skill and preferences. Rather, this is how it had to be because of technical limitations, and then the rest of the game was designed to accommodate these shortcomings.

To take yet another example, in section 4, I explained the algorithms behind a typical enemy in a first-person shooter through describing its seven-second "life span." Why only seven seconds? Early first-person shooters were designed with essentially no persistent characters in order to mask their simplicity. If you interacted with a character in *DOOM* for a minute, its simplistic programming would be painfully obvious for every player. But if the enemy is on screen for only a few seconds, there aren't enough clues for you as to how intelligent it is (or isn't). And later first-person shooters were heavily influenced by the trailblazers of the genre, such as *DOOM* (figure 8.1).

In other words, video games of that era were designed around the lack of AI. This led to a number of design choices that would not have been made had better AI been available. For example, boss fights were designed around patterns of recurring actions

Figure 8.1
DOOM (id Software, 1993) was one of the original first-person shooters and a major influence in the development of this game genre.

that the player needed to decode instead of around the boss trying to genuinely outsmart the player and dialogues in role-playing games were designed around a set of fixed dialogue choices rather than around NPCs having a dynamic knowledge base about the world that the player character could query in arbitrary ways. For the same reasons, difficulty scaling in games is typically implemented through giving computer-controlled adversaries more or fewer resources, essentially cheating rather than modeling the player's skill and adapting the depth of decision making of the computer-controlled characters.

These design choices came to define game genres as other designers copied them and players started expecting them. It is possible to break the genre conventions, but this may involve creating new genres. Creating a role-playing game that does not have fixed dialogue trees, as the AI researcher Michael Mateas and game developer Andrew Stern did in their groundbreaking relationship drama game *Façade*, has come to be seen as creating a new type of game rather than trying to repair an aspect of role-playing game design that has been broken since the beginning. Given the (justifiable) cautiousness of most large game developers and publishers, it is no wonder that the rather remarkable recent advances in AI methods are barely reflected at all in game development. Existing games do not need advanced AI because they are designed not to need it.

AI-Based Game Design Patterns

For someone like me, who cares deeply about both artificial intelligence and games, the natural question is how to change this. Advances in AI methods promise to make amazing new games possible, but because of conservative design and development practices, this is not yet happening. So how can we design games that actually need advanced AI methods?

That was the question a handful of my colleagues and I posed one cold January day in the attic of Schloss Dagstuhl, a German castle where we were organizing a seminar on the future of AI in games. We decided to investigate the different roles AI can play in games, trying to find examples from well-known or little-known games that use AI in such a way that you need to interact with and understand it to play the game well. We tried to categorize these into design patterns. The design patterns we came up with,[1] some of which follow, could serve as inspiration for envisioning even more ways of designing around AI.

AI Is Visualized: In this design pattern, the internal workings of the AI algorithm are exposed to the player, and the player can use that information in game play. In other words, the player can see how one or several NPCs think by looking inside its mind. An example is the stealth game *Third Eye Crime*, where you are tasked with outsmarting security guards. The guard behavior is driven by an AI technique called occupancy maps, which create a model of where the guards should explore next as they go looking for you. The trick here is that these occupancy maps are visible to the player through being laid out on the game map. In effect, the player can see the state of the guards' minds (figure 8.2). In order to play the game well, the player needs to understand the AI system to predict what the NPCs will do.

AI as Role Model: Many of the algorithms that underlie NPC behavior are relatively simple and easy to predict, as we saw in chapter 4. Instead of trying to make these algorithms more human-like, one intriguing game design idea is to make humans behave more like the algorithms. *Spy Party* is an asymmetric

Figure 8.2
In *Third Eye Crime* (Moonshot Games, 2014), the colors on the ground signal to the player both where the guards can currently see and where they are thinking of looking next, offering the player a view into the mind of the enemy.

two-player game, where one player has to identify a human player in a group of NPCs and the other player tries to blend in as much as possible so as not to be identified by the first player while carrying out a mission that has been assigned to her. Blending in is best accomplished by trying to copy NPCs' movement patterns and decision making (figure 8.3). In other words, one player needs to understand how the algorithms that drive the NPCs' behavior works through observation in order to copy the behavior, and the other player needs to understand the same behavior in order to discern the interloping human. One way of seeing this game mechanic is as a form of reverse Turing test. The basic concept behind the Turing test is highly appealing and

Figure 8.3
A scene from *Spy Party* (Chris Hecker, 2009) features a number of NPCs in a bar, and one player must try to blend in seamlessly with them.

it's possible that many other interesting game mechanics could be built on it.

AI as Trainee: The god game (or management simulator game, if you want a more mundane name for this genre) *Black and White* puts the player in the role of a local deity, in various ways influencing the life of mostly hapless villagers (figure 8.4). The most important way to influence the villager is through a giant creature, which acts as your embodied stand-in in the world. You cannot control this creature directly; instead you must teach it how to interact with the villagers. You do this by rewarding and punishing it for its actions and by showing it by example what to do. The creature's behavior is driven by machine learning algorithms, which learn from your actions in real time as you play the game. To play this game well, you need to master the art of training the creature, which is a little bit like learning to train a dog: you can do it without understanding very much of what actually goes on in the dog's head.

Figure 8.4
The giant creatures in *Black and White* (Lionhead Studios, 2001) can do your bidding, but only if you train them well.

Another take on this particular pattern is to build games where you train agents that are then competing or fighting against each other, a little bit like the training mechanic of the *Pokémon* series but with actual machine learning instead of a simple role-playing game-style progress mechanic. One example of this is *NERO* (NeuroEvolution of Robotic Operatives), a research-based game by Ken Stanley, now at University of Central Florida and Uber AI Labs. In that game, you train an army of miniature soldiers through designing various tasks for them and deciding what kind of behavior to reward them for.[2] Another research game from my team, *EvoCommander*, is based on the same idea of training agents to do the player's bidding,

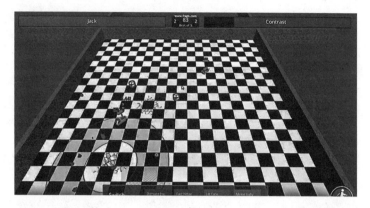

Figure 8.5
A family tree of brains in *EvoCommander* (Daniel Jallov, 2015). Before a match, you choose which of your trained brains to bring with you into battle.

but instead of training multiple agents, you train a number of "brains" (separate neural networks) for a simulated robot (figure 8.5). When playing against another player, you then control the robot indirectly through selecting which brain it should use at each point in time.[3]

AI Is Editable: You can also design a game around directly editing the instructions for the algorithms that control the behavior of an agent. The board game *RoboRally* is proof of the possibility of creating a very successful game around such a mechanic. In *RoboRally*, each player in turn chooses the instructions that her robot should carry out in that turn. Although the "programming" here is simplistic, predicting the resultant behavior is very challenging because all players' robots carry out their programs in parallel.

A more advanced example is the network editor mode of *Galactic Arms Race*, another research-based game by Ken

Stanley's team. *Galactic Arms Race* is a third-person space shooter game built around a unique form of search-based procedural content generation (figure 8.6). Weapons in this game are controlled by neural networks, which decide how the particles fired by the player's spaceship behave. Players can collect and discard weapons throughout the game world, and at any point, they can switch between several equipped weapons. Weapons are created through a collaborative evolutionary algorithm where all players of the game act as a fitness function; new weapons are the offspring of the weapons that players choose to use the most. This is in itself a very interesting use of AI techniques in the game, though more in a background role because players do not need to understand the weapon-generating evolutionary algorithm to play the game. The AI-is-editable design pattern was introduced in an extension to the game, which makes it possible to manually edit the neural networks defining the weapons. The structure of neural networks is generally hard to understand for humans, meaning that this editing mode is not for everyone, but for some players, editing the neural network to try to get a desired weapon behavior is an engaging puzzle game in itself.[4]

AI Is Guided: Yet another idea for how to design a game around AI so that the player needs to interact with and understand it is to have game characters controlled by AI algorithms, but imperfectly so either because you limit what the algorithms can do or because the tasks the game characters are asked to perform are too complex. The player will then need to act as a guide or manager for the agents, giving them high-level commands or guiding them through operations they cannot perform by themselves. An excellent example of this design pattern is the enormously successful *The Sims* series of games. These games can best be described as life simulators or virtual dollhouses, where

Figure 8.6
Evolved weapons in *Galactic Arms Race* (Evolutionary Games, 2009).

you control a family of characters as they go about their life. You need to make all the large life decisions for them, such as where to build a house, but in many cases you also need to help out with small tasks, such as making sure there are pots and pans available for cooking. But the characters also have a say. *The Sims* games feature complex AI systems that control the agent, so that they not only perform autonomous actions such as going to the bathroom and cooking dinner but also strike up friendships and fall in love (figure 8.7). Playing the game is a constant balancing act between the player and the AI system. Crucially the game frequently communicates the state of its AI systems via little thought bubbles above the characters' heads, allowing the player to understand what goes on.

Figure 8.7
A romantic encounter in *The Sims 4* (Maxis, 2013).

Of course, this is just a small subset of the many, many possible ways in which AI can be used in visible roles within video games. And I have mentioned only one pattern involving procedural generation and none building on player modeling. It is pretty clear that there is a vast and underexplored design space out there, with plenty of novel game design ideas available for those who look beyond established genres and preconceptions on what parts AI can and cannot play.

9 General Intelligence and Games in General

Let us return to the question of what intelligence actually is, the one I discussed in chapter 3 without coming to any satisfying conclusion. Since you are reading this, you clearly haven't given up on reading this book, but you may be a bit disappointed with me because I apparently can't give you a straight answer. Well, I was just being honest. It is still very much up for debate to what extent there exists such a thing as general intelligence. I won't try to force a particular view on you because I think there's plenty of work, both philosophical and empirical, left to do to understand this question better. What it seems we can all agree on, however, is that some artificial intelligence systems have broader applicability than others in the sense that they can perform a wider range of tasks and that it is a desirable quality of an AI system to be generic rather than specific. There is nothing wrong with AI systems that can do only one thing if we are simply trying to engineer a solution to a specific problem. If we are trying to make scientific progress on creating artificial intelligence, however, then it is important that we build systems that can do a range of different things—for example, play different games.

Around the time that I was finishing my PhD, I thought that the little car racing game I had constructed for my experiments with evolving neural networks was pretty nifty and that other people might want to use it for their own experiments, so I decided to make the code available. As I was doing that, I decided to start a competition. Researchers, students, and anyone else could submit their best agents, and they would compete against each other. Just like in real-world car racing, the car that finished the course fastest would win. Also just like in real-world car racing, the collisions were the most fun part to watch. I quickly got a few dozen competitors from all over the world, submitting controllers based on some pretty different AI techniques. The winner used a technique called *fuzzy logic* to reason about how to drive best, but there were several good agents based on reinforcement learning and evolutionary algorithms. Seeing how well the competition went, I decided to run it again, but this time I teamed up with some Italian researchers, Pier Luca Lanzi and Daniele Loiacono at the Politecnico di Milano, to move it over to a more capable 3D racing game called *TORCS*. The competition ran for seven years, with continued participation from universities, and in some cases hobbyists and private companies, around the world (figure 9.1).[1]

A few years later I started another AI competition based on *Infinite Mario*, the open-source clone of *Super Mario Bros.* I mentioned earlier. My student Sergey Karakovskiy and I rebuilt *Infinite Mario* into an AI benchmark and had people submit their best Mario-playing AI agents. With a few weeks to go before the end of the competition, a young PhD student by the name of Robin Baumgarten submitted an agent based on the A* algorithm discussed in chapter 4. The agent was stupendously effective. It completed all the levels our level generators could

Figure 9.1
TORCS, 2014. (Image courtesy of the Libre Game Wiki.)

generate seemingly faultlessly and went on to win the competition. This was a bit of a letdown for us, as we had imagined that we had constructed a hard AI problem, only for an agent based on such a simple and well-known algorithm to walk all over it. In an attempt to salvage the competition for the next round, we went to work on making the level generator meaner. Next time we ran the competition, the level generator created levels with frequent dead ends, which Mario would need to backtrack to get out of. This was a challenge that Baumgarten's A* agent could not overcome; instead, the next competition was won by a complex agent called REALM, which combined evolutionary algorithms with a rule-based system and, as one subservient part of the mix, an A* algorithm similar to Baumgarten's.[2]

Of course, I was not the first to run game-based AI competitions. Competitions for AI players of Chess, Checkers, and Go have been running for decades. Within the video game space, there have been long-running AI competitions based on classic arcade games such *Ms. Pac-Man*, first-person shooters such as *DOOM*, and physics puzzle games such as *Angry Birds*. One of the most active competitions right now is the *StarCraft* competition, which revolves around a game in which the best submitted agents still stand no chance against a good human player.

In most of these competitions, as least those that continue for a few years, there is clear progress. Racing agents submitted to the 2012 Simulated Car Racing Competition literally run laps around those submitted to the 2008 competition, and agents submitted to the 2011 Mario AI Competition finish levels that agents submitted to the 2009 competition would not. This is all good and would seem to suggest that these competitions spur advancements in game-playing AI. Looking at the submissions from each year, however, you can see a worrying trend: there are, in general, fewer and fewer *general* AI algorithms in the later submissions. The submissions to the first edition of Simulated Car Racing Competition consisted of agents using relatively general-purpose algorithms that could have been used to play other games with minor changes. In later years of the competition, agents were being tailored more and more to the task of playing this particular racing game, including painstakingly handcrafted mechanisms for changing gears, learning the shape of the track, blocking overtaking cars, and so on. In fact, machine learning algorithms in general were used in fewer and lesser roles in later years' submissions compared to those at the beginning of the competitions. Advanced AI algorithms were demoted to supporting roles. The improvement in the agents' performance is not really due to any improvements in the underlying algorithms but to better game-specific engineering. A similar development could be observed in the Mario AI competition. As for the *Star-Craft* competitions, the agents that win tend to be intricately handcrafted strategies with little in the way of what we would normally call AI, such as search or machine learning algorithms.

Above all, these agents are very specific. The agents submitted to the *Mario* AI Competition cannot control the cars in the Simulated Car Racing Competition or build bases and command armies in *StarCraft*. The *StarCraft* agents cannot drive cars or play *Super Mario Bros.*, and so on. It's not just that the agent would play these games badly; it's that it cannot play them at all: the game state is represented very differently for each of the game. The *StarCraft* game state makes no sense to the *Mario*-playing agent, and the outputs of that agent (such as running and jumping) make no sense to the *StarCraft* game.

This is not a problem unique to these competitions. I mentioned back in chapter 5 that DeepMind trained neural networks to play a few dozen classic Atari games. This might seem like an example of more general game-playing AI, were it not for the fact that each neural network is trained to play one game only. The neural network trained to play *Space Invaders* cannot play *Pac-Man*, *Montezuma's Revenge*, or any of the other Atari games— at least not play them any better than the proverbial monkey in front of a typewriter, but with a joystick instead of a typewriter. There have been several attempts to train neural networks to be able to play more than one game, so far with limited success.[3] The same thing is true for the other famous game-playing agent from DeepMind, AlphaGo. It is very good at playing Go, but it can only play Go. It can't play anything else, not even Chess.[4]

General Video Game Playing

Let's return to the question of developing general artificial intelligence, or at least somewhat general artificial intelligence. It seems all this work on developing AI agents that can play individual games may not be moving us that much closer to this goal after all. In the worst case, it may even be a case of two steps forward and one step backward: we keep spending resources on understanding and exploiting the dynamics of individual games rather than trying to create agents that can demonstrate more general intelligence. The best way to demonstrate more general intelligence would be for the same agent, with no or little retraining, to solve multiple different tasks, such as playing multiple different games.

How would you ensure that researchers work on creating agents that have some more general game-playing capacity? You create a competition! That's what a group of us were thinking back in 2013 as we started working on the General Video Game AI (GVG-AI) Competition (figure 9.2) The idea was to have a competition where you cannot tailor your agent to a particular game, so you have to make it at least somewhat general. We figured that we needed to design the competition so you did not know what games your agent was going to play. Every time we ran the competition, we needed new games that no one had seen before (even though they could be similar to or versions of well-known games). For this, we needed a way to easily create these games, so we started by designing a new language specifically for creating games in the style of classic arcade games. Tom Schaul took the lead in creating this language, which we call the Video Game Description Language (VGDL). Diego Perez-Liebana then took the lead in creating the competition software.

So far, we've run the GVG-AI competition a few times per year since 2014. Every competition event tests all the submitted agents on a set of ten new games, which must be handmade for each competition. To date, more than a hundred games have been created, many of them versions of or inspired by arcade

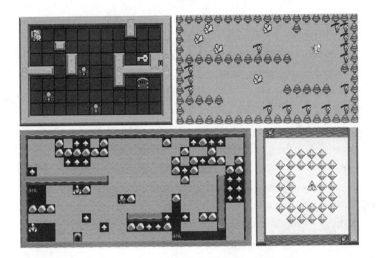

Figure 9.2
Four different games in the GVG-AI framework: *Zelda*, *Butterflies*, *Boulder Dash*, and *Solar Fox*. The common interface means that the same agent can play all games in the framework, but with varying skill.

games from the 1980s. Competitors don't know which games their agents will be tested on until after they have submitted their agents, making sure that they spend their energy on improving the agents' general game-playing capacities rather than their fit with a particular game. Currently, the best agents can reliably win at fewer than half of the existing games, showing that there is ample room for improvement.[5]

If someone constructed an agent that could win at all of the existing games in the GVG-AI competition, would we call that agent "generally intelligent"? Well, not quite yet. The GVG-AI software gives the AI agents access to a forward model, or a simulator of the games, which makes it easy to plan your actions by simulating what would happen if you executed your plan.

For example, the version of the A* agent that won the *Mario* AI competition crucially depends on having a forward model. You would generally not have access to that as a human playing classic arcade games, and the "real world" notoriously lacks a forward model. We are working on a new version of the competition, which does not provide agents with this possibility but instead gives them a short amount of time to adapt to each game. Also, the games that can be expressed in the current version of VGDL are limited to the kinds of games you would find in an early 1980s home computer or arcade hall, and even then some types of games are missing (e.g., there are no text-based games). In some unspecified future, we hope that VGDL or some successor language will be able to express a much wider range of games. We also hope that at some point in the future, it will be possible to generate these games automatically, making it much easier to create new games to test AI agents on.

While the GVG-AI project is only a small step toward solving, or even properly formulating, the problem of general game playing, I do believe that it is extremely relevant for understanding intelligence in general. As we have seen in the book, games are incredibly diverse, and they challenge our cognitive capacities in ways we are barely beginning to understand. If at some point in the future we create an agent that can learn quickly to play all video games or even just the most well-designed ones (let's say the top 100 popular games on each of the major distribution platforms, such as Steam or the iOS App Store) with a skill similar to that of a game-playing human, then I think we will have achieved artificial general intelligence. At the very least, we will have enormously advanced our understanding of what intelligence is and is not.

10 Synthesis

I regret to inform you that the book is almost over now. I know this is a little bit sad—for you, not for me. It took a lot of effort to write this book, and I'm happy that I'm basically done. It all started with my cats being rehomed, and ten chapters later, we have explored game design, definitions of intelligence, narrow and general artificial intelligence, automatic creativity, and games that learn who you are and what you want, among other things. In order to structure the closing comments, we will here revisit the three broad claims that I made at the beginning of the book and outline how the discussion in the book supports these claims.

Games are the future of AI. Games provide the best benchmarks for AI because of the way they are designed to challenge many different human cognitive abilities, as well as for their technical convenience and the availability of human data. We have only began to scratch the surface of game-based AI benchmarks.

Games, especially well-designed games, are fantastic AI benchmarks because they are designed to test our cognitive capacities; they are engaging to play partly because they are unusually pedagogical intelligence tests. We have seen how board games have been used as AI benchmarks since the very beginning of AI research, but also how landmark achievements such as Deep Blue and AlphaGo have made board games less relevant for future AI testing. To some extent, the classic board games are simply done. Attention is shifting to video games, which provide a different and in many ways much richer set of challenges; the diversity of video games means that all the broad cognitive abilities from Cattell-Horn-Carroll theory are challenged by some video games. Many video games, including real-time strategy games such as *StarCraft*, are also much harder than any of the classic board games for various reasons, such as large branching factors and hidden information. But it's not enough to create agents that play individual video games well. If we want to create more general artificial intelligence—which most agree is a central goal of AI, despite the disagreement over what intelligence is—we need to create agents that can play any games we present them with. For this, we need benchmarks and competitions that reflect the real diversity of video games. To make this feasible, we will probably need to generate these games at least partly automatically.

AI is the future of games. We now have much more capable AI methods than just a few years ago, and we are rapidly learning how to best apply them to games. The potential roles of AI in games go far beyond providing skillful opponents. We need to adapt our ways of thinking about game design to fully harness the power of advanced AI algorithms and enable a new generation of AI-augmented games.

There is a sizeable gulf between the AI methods that are being researched in academia and the AI methods employed in most games. While there exist some sophisticated techniques for controlling NPCs in games, more general-purpose AI methods are largely absent from commercial game development. Compared to other industries, game development is curiously unaffected by the current surge of interest in artificial intelligence. This is to a large extent because most game genres build on design blueprints that were laid down decades ago, when effective AI on consumer hardware was more or less impossible. Games are therefore designed to not need AI. To change this and harness some of the possibilities modern AI brings, we need to rethink game design, starting with the roles that AI can play. There are many unexplored roles for AI beyond standard NPC control. One particularly prominent role for AI algorithms is that of generating game content. Procedural content generation has been a feature of some games for decades, but new methods based on, for example, evolutionary algorithms make much more wide-ranging and controllable content generation possible. Player modeling is another key use case for AI in games, and modeling players' preferences and behavior makes it possible to adapt games to particular players, suggesting a future where games could continuously reinvent themselves in response to what players do. They may even invent content players do not realize they want yet. Tools such as player modeling and content generation can also be useful for designers and make game development easier and more accessible. All these methods are, however, dependent on progress in AI agents that can play games in general.

Games and AI for games help us understand intelligence. By studying how humans play and design games, we can understand how they think, and we can attempt to replicate this thinking by creating game-playing and game-designing AI agents. Game design is a cognitive science; it studies thinking—human thinking and machine thinking.

The fact that some games are easy for humans to play but hard for current algorithms, and vice versa, is an important source of information on our thinking. It tells us how our thinking differs from that of the algorithms we currently have and can inspire us to create new AI methods. But it's not only in the context of game playing that game AI can inform us about thinking. Algorithms for designing games, or parts of games, can be seen as models of human creativity. Trying to create software that can design games will give us some idea of how human creative processes, currently badly understood, work. And the differences between human and machine design will tell us more about this process and give us ideas for further creative algorithms.

Finally, I'll reiterate that all of the research topics discussed in this book feed into each other. AI for games and games for AI are not the same thing, but advances in one of these endeavors will enable advances in the other. And there is much left to do in this young research field with so many open research questions in every direction. It is also an inherently interdisciplinary research field, where computer scientists, cognitive scientists, designers, and humanities scholars who care about games can contribute.

Perhaps you would like to join us?

Further Reading

I hope that this book has inspired you to read more about its topics and maybe even dive into this research field yourself. Throughout the book, I have included a number of notes with references to papers that expand on each topic in greater detail. The papers may be more or less accessible given your technical background, so you might want a more coherent introduction to some topics. To that end, here I offer some book recommendations.

Georgios Yannakakis and I recently published *Artificial Intelligence and Games* (2018), a textbook that covers approximately the same topics as this book but from a much more technical angle. Read it to learn the algorithms behind the discussions in this book. The book presupposes a computer science background, including an understanding of the fundamentals of artificial intelligence.

If you are specifically interested in the topics of chapter 7, I recommend the book *Procedural Content Generation in Games* (2016), edited and cowritten by Noor Shaker, Mark Nelson, and me, with contributions from a dozen or so leading researchers in the field. This is also a technical book.

If you want to learn the basics of artificial intelligence, the standard work is *Artificial Intelligence: A Modern Approach* (2009) by Stuart Russell and Peter Norvig. It's a great reference because of its completeness, but that's not saying it's the most accessible book there is. Many online courses on the basics of AI may be more accessible introductions. There are some good introductory books for certain subfields of AI. *Deep Learning with Python* (2017) by François Chollet is a highly accessible and useful introduction to modern neural network techniques. *Introduction to Evolutionary Computing* (2003) by A. E. Eiben and J. E. Smith is a good introduction to and overview of evolutionary computation, which has been used in much of the work described in this book. There are also many good books on game design and game studies, some of them practical books about the game design process and others geared more toward describing the space of game designs in a more formal and abstract way. In the latter category, two books that I have found useful when thinking about (artificial) intelligence and games are *Rules of Play: Game Design Fundamentals* (2004) by Katie Salen Tekinbaş and Eric Zimmerman and *Characteristics of Games* (2012) by George Skaff Elias, Richard Garfield, and K. Robert Gutschera. Beyond books, Tommy Thompson has produced a great series of accessible videos on AI and games that are available on YouTube and on http://aiandgames.com.

Like all of artificial intelligence, the AI and games field moves fast. If you want to keep up to date, you can peruse the proceedings (freely available online) of the main conferences: IEEE Conference on Computational Intelligence and Games (CIG) and AAAI Conference on Artificial Intelligence and Interactive Digital Entertainment (AIIDE). Additionally, many relevant papers are published in the proceedings of the Foundations of

Digital Games (FDG) conference and its associated workshops, such as the Procedural Content Generation Workshop. Another important publication is *IEEE Transactions on Games*, a journal that publishes technical and scientific research on games including AI. Nowadays, papers are typically uploaded to repositories such as ArXiv before they are published, often even before they are submitted for publication. Given the enormous volume of papers that are submitted to ArXiv, the best way of finding out about interesting papers posted online is probably to follow researchers on Twitter. You can start with @togelius.

Notes

Prologue: AI&I

1. Math and I are still not the best of friends. Contrary to popular misconceptions, you do not need to be mathematically inclined to have a successful career in computer science.

What Is This Book?

1. But I've tried to keep the footnotes short.

Chapter 1: In the Beginning of AI, There Were Games

1. Turing wrote an account of this event in Turing et al. (1953).

2. Samuel (1959).

3. For more about this match and the system that won it, see Campbell, Hoane, and Hsu (2002). It is worth noting that the development of better computer Chess software has by no means ceased, and that computers have also kept getting faster; you can now download software for your laptop that will play Chess better than any human player out there.

4. Of course, both East Asia and Europe comprise many cultures, but both of these games have historically been popular in many countries across these regions.

5. For a thorough introduction to MCTS, see the popular survey paper by Browne and Maire (2010).

6. Silver et al. (2016).

7. Computers achieved superhuman performance on several other games much earlier, and some games, such as Checkers have even been "solved," meaning that the computer can play a provably perfect game against any opponent (Schaeffer et al., 2007).

Chapter 2: Do You Need to Be Intelligent to Play Games?

1. The theory is described in Carroll (2003).

2. Koster's book, *A Theory of Fun for Game Design* (2005), is surprisingly fun to read.

3. In their excellent book *Characteristics of Games*, Elias, Garfield, and Gutschera (2012) describe heuristic accumulation at some length. I have tried to lay out how the chain of heuristics relates to the depth of a game (Lantz et al., 2017).

4. Vygotsky (1978).

5. Csikszentmihalyi (1990). There have also been attempts to develop offshoots of the flow theory specifically tailored to games (Sweetser and Wyeth, 2005).

6. This theory has been developed in a number of publications and applied to various machine learning tasks, but for a readable overview, see Schmidhuber (2006).

Chapter 3: What Is (Artificial) Intelligence?

1. For a more thorough overview of various definitions of intelligence from the perspective of artificial intelligence, see Legg and Hutter (2007).

2. Turing was a coinventor of the computer, genius mathematician, war hero, LGBT martyr, and many other things. See Hodges (2012) for an excellent biography.

3. The paper where the test was proposed is Turing (1950). It's a fascinating paper full of intriguing arguments, and very readable; most of it does not require any particular technical background. Bring it to the beach next time you go, and enjoy it with a cold beer.

4. Interestingly, it seems that the Turing test is getting harder to pass as time passes. The computer program Eliza was invented in the 1960s as a parody of Rogerian nondirectional psychotherapy, as well as a contribution to natural language processing. You can interact with Eliza by "chatting" with it, but most of the program's answers will be either reformulations of what you said or very general questions such as, "Tell me about your mother." When the program was announced to the public, many of those who tried it would not believe it was a computer program because they could not believe that a computer could say these things. They were sure there must be a human "at the other end." These days, very few people would be fooled by Eliza. People are used to the existence of chatbots, and many have interacted with them over Twitter or Slack or as part of a game. Young people in particular would quickly see through Eliza's antics.

5. As of the time of writing, I am thirty-eight years old and still have not gotten myself a driver's license.

6. Imagine a game that had a million different moves available each turn, all with different outcomes but with no obvious visualization to let you choose among them. The ordering and names of the moves changed every turn. You would not be able to play this any better than if you played randomly, whereas a computer could easily simulate the outcome of each move and play the game well.

7. This is the title of one of his papers, and a pretty readable one too (Brooks, 1990).

8. The paper is Legg and Hutter (2007). Legg went on to cofound Deep-Mind, which Google later bought for a very respectable sum and is currently the world's preeminent AI research lab.

9. Though it took just over fifty years from the Wright flyer to the Apollo rocket.

10. Turing (1950).

Chapter 4: Do Video Games Have Artificial Intelligence?

1. The word *state* is here used similarly to how we use it for humans or dogs: Fido could be bored, hungry, happy, or sleeping. Technically, the state of a game character is a particular configuration of the variables that define the character. It is related to but different from the use in chapter 2, where we talked about the "game state," which is all the variables that define the game.

2. Actually, the one where the sum of the distance already traveled and the estimated distance to the goal is lowest.

3. For more about A* algorithms and some of the myriad variations, see any standard AI textbook, such as Russell and Norvig (2009). For more on finite state machines and behavior trees, see a dedicated game AI textbook, such as Millington and Funge (2009).

4. Jeff Orkin, the AI lead developer of *F.E.A.R.*, wrote about the planning system in an influential paper (Orkin, 2006). Damian Isla (2005) similarly wrote about some important aspects of the AI of *Halo 2*. The *Shadow of Mordor* system has been discussed in talks at the Game Developers Conference, but nothing has been published about it in the academic literature as far as I know.

5. The subjective experience of artificial agents is a can of worms that we are not quite ready to open. Those worms are doing just fine inside the can for now.

6. According the classification in Elias et al. (2012), it (and many other games we usually refer to as single player) is really a one-and-a-half-player game, as it lets a human play against AI opponents. For simplicity, I will continue calling such games single-player games in this book.

7. Ontanón et al. (2013) is a good overview of the state of the art of AI versus AI *StarCraft* competitions.

Chapter 5: Growing a Mind and Learning to Play

1. Like many others, I came to the field of AI as a romantic and was molded into a utilitarian. The romantic streak is still there, though, and breaks out at uneven intervals.

2. Darwin (1859).

3. Indeed, not entirely unlike the so-bad-it's-good "series of tubes" metaphor for the Internet alluded to by Senator Ted Stevens.

4. Back when I started this line of research, I did not have a driving license and I lived outside the sleepy town of Colchester, England. I still don't have a driving license, but I have since moved to New York City. I keep thinking I should get myself a driving license before all cars drive themselves, so I'll have to learn to drive in Manhattan. It appears I like playing this game at a high difficulty level.

5. Mnih et al. (2015).

Chapter 6: Do Games Learn from You When You Play Them?

1. It is sometimes said that while astronomy and other branches of physics deal with large numbers, computer science deals with *really* large numbers. This is just how combinatorics works. Remember that six digits between 0 and 9 can be combined in a million ways (all the numbers you can write between 000000 and 999999). Similarly, if your game state is represented by 1,000 bytes (a kilobyte) of memory, then you have about 10^{2456} possible game states. Yes, that's one followed by 2,456 zeroes.

2. Bartle's original paper (1996) is refers to multiuser dungeons (MUDs) but has since been used to talk about and classify players across essentially all game genres (Bartle, 1996).

3. Drachen, Canossa, and Yannakakis (2009).

4. Mahlmann et al. (2010).

5. Canossa, Martinez, and Togelius (2013).

6. Yee, Ducheneaut, Nelson, and Likarish (2011).

7. This research is reported in a number of papers, including Tekofsky, Van Den Herik, Spronck, and Plaat (2013), and Tekofsky, Spronck, Goudbeek, Plaat, and van den Herik (2015).

Chapter 7: Automating Creativity

1. The main paper to come out of this project was Togelius, De Nardi, and Lucas (2007).

2. In this case, we were inspired by the work of Thomas Malone (1981) and Raph Koster (2005).

3. The idea of search-based procedural content generation is laid out in more detail in Togelius, Yannakakis, Stanley, and Brown (2011). For the work on *StarCraft* maps and *Super Mario Bros*, see Togelius et al. (2013) and Dahlskog and Togelius (2014), respectively. An interestingly different take on seeing content generation as search is to use a constraint solver, as demonstrated in Smith and Mateas (2010) and Smith, Whitehead, and Mateas. (2011).

4. Boden (1991).

5. The research described in this section was reported in several papers, of which Pedersen, Togelius, and Yannakakis (2010) and Shaker, Yannakakis, and Togelius (2010) are the most important; there's also an overview paper about the experience-driven approach (Yannakakis and Togelius, 2011).

6. Browne and Maire (2010).

7. Togelius and Schmidhuber (2008).

8. Nielsen, Barros, Togelius, and Nelson (2015).

9. Smith and Mateas (2010).

10. See, for example, Cook and Colton (2011, 2014).

11. Smith et al. (2011).

12. Liapis, Yannakakis, and Togelius (2013).

13. With various collaborators, I have, for example, worked on the *Ropossum* tool for AI-assisted level generation in the popular physics-based puzzle game *Cut the Rope* (Shaker, Shaker, and Togelius, 2013) and an AI-assisted tool for creating game rules in the video game description language (Machado, Nealen, and Togelius, 2017). Another interesting example is the AI-assisted level editor for the puzzle game *Refraction* (Butler, Smith, Liu, and Popvic, 2013).

Chapter 8: Designing for AI

1. The rest of this chapter largely builds on the paper that came out of that long discussion in the German castle attic (Treanor et al., 2015). That paper lists more patterns than this chapter and also contains two game prototypes mean to illustrate and explore further such patterns.

2. Stanley, Bryant, and Miikkulainen (2005).

3. Jallov, Risi, and Togelius (2017).

4. The Galactic Arms Race game is described in Hastings, Guha, and Stanley (2009), and the neural network editing extension is described in Hastings and Stanley (2010).

Chapter 9: General Intelligence and Games in General

1. We wrote a paper summarizing the competitors and results of the first competition (Togelius et al., 2008) and, later, a similar paper about the new car racing competition (Loiacono et al., 2010).

2. The paper describing the game-playing track of the Mario AI Competition, as we called it, is Karakovskiy and Togelius (2012). The REALM agent is described in Bojarski and Congdon (2010).

3. The original paper is Mnih et al. (2015); one of the several attempts at creating more generally capable agents is Rusu et al. (2016).

4. A recent development of AlphaGo called *AlphaZero* uses a similar combination of reinforcement learning and tree search to learn to play not just Go but also Chess and the Go-related game Shogi. However, it trains separate networks for each game and even uses different representation of the board state for the different games, so the Go-playing network cannot play Chess or Shogi (Silver et al., 2017).

5. The GVG-AI competition and some of its results are described in Perez-Liebana, Samothrakis, Togelius, Lucas, et al. (2016), and Perez-Liebana, Samothrakis, Togelius, Schaul, et al. (2016). The GVG-AI project was also inspired by the earlier General Game Playing competition, which focuses on board games (Genesereth, Love, and Pell, 2005).

Bibliography

Boden, M. A. (1991). *The creative mind: Myths and mechanisms*. New York, NY: Basic Books.

Bojarski, S., & Congdon, C. B. (2010). Realm: A rule-based evolutionary computation agent that learns to play *Mario*. In *Proceedings of the 2010 IEEE Symposium on Computational Intelligence and Games* (pp. 83–90). Piscataway, NJ: IEEE.

Brooks, R. A. (1990). Elephants don't play chess. *Robotics and Autonomous Systems*, 6(1–2), 3–15.

Browne, C., & Maire, F. (2010). Evolutionary game design. *IEEE Transactions on Computational Intelligence and AI in Games*, 2(1), 1–16.

Browne, C., Powley, E., Whitehouse, D., Lucas, S., Cowling, P., Rohlfshagen, P., ... Colton, S. (2012). A survey of Monte Carlo tree search methods. *IEEE Transactions on Computational Intelligence and AI in Games*, 4(1), 1–43.

Butler, E., Smith, A. M., Liu, Y.-E., & Popovic, Z. (2013). A mixed-initiative tool for designing level progressions in games. In *Proceedings of the 26th Annual ACM Symposium on User Interface Software and Technology* (pp. 377–386). New York, NY: ACM.

Campbell, M., Hoane, A. J., & Hsu, F.-H. (2002). Deep Blue. *Artificial Intelligence*, 134(1–2), 57–83.

Canossa, A., Martinez, J. B., & Togelius, J. (2013). Give me a reason to dig: *Minecraft* and psychology of motivation. In *Proceedings of the 2013 IEEE Conference on Computational Intelligence and Games* (pp. 1–8). Piscataway, NJ: IEEE.

Carroll, J. B. (2003). The higher-stratum structure of cognitive abilities: Current evidence supports *g* and about ten broad factors. In H. Nyborg (Ed.), *The scientific study of general intelligence: Tribute to Arthur Jensen* (pp. 5–21) Amsterdam, Netherlands: Elsevier.

Chollet, F. (2017). *Deep learning with Python*. Shelter Island, NY: Manning Publications Company.

Cook, M., & Colton, S. (2011). Multi-faceted evolution of simple arcade games. In *Proceedings of the 2011 IEEE Conference on Computational Intelligence and Games* (pp. 289–296). Piscataway, NJ: IEEE.

Cook, M., & Colton, S. (2014). *Ludus ex machina: Building a 3D game designer that competes alongside humans*. Paper presented at the Fifth International Conference on Computational Creativity, Ljubljana, Slovenia, June 10–13.

Csikszentmihalyi, M. (1990). *Flow: The psychology of optimal experience*. New York, NY: Harper & Row.

Dahlskog, S., & Togelius, J. (2014). Procedural content generation using patterns as objectives. In *Proceedings of the European Conference on the Applications of Evolutionary Computation* (pp. 325–336). Cham, Switzerland: Springer.

Darwin, C. (1859). *On the origin of species by means of natural selection, or the preservation of favoured races in the struggle for life*. London: Murray.

Drachen, A., Canossa, A., & Yannakakis, G. N. (2009). Player modeling using self-organization in *Tomb Raider: Underworld*. In *Proceedings of the 2009 IEEE Symposium on Computational Intelligence and Games* (pp. 1–8). Piscataway, NJ: IEEE.

Eiben, A. E., & Smith, J. E. (2003). *Introduction to evolutionary computing*. Cham, Switzerland: Springer.

Elias, G. S., Garfield, R., & Gutschera, K. R. (2012). *Characteristics of games*. Cambridge, MA: MIT Press.

Genesereth, M., Love, N., & Pell, B. (2005). General game playing: Overview of the AAAI competition. *AI Magazine*, 26(2), 62.

Hastings, E. J., Guha, R. K., & Stanley, K. O. (2009). Automatic content generation in the *Galactic Arms Race* video game. *IEEE Transactions on Computational Intelligence and AI in Games*, 1(4), 245–263.

Hastings, E. J., & Stanley, K. O. (2010). *Interactive genetic engineering of evolved video game content*. Paper presented at the 2010 Workshop on Procedural Content Generation in Games, Monterey, CA, June 18.

Hodges, A. (2012). *Alan Turing: The enigma*. New York, NY: Random House.

Isla, D. (2005). *Managing complexity in the Halo 2 AI system*. Paper presented at the 2005 Game Developers Conference, San Francisco, CA, March.

Jallov, D., Risi, S., & Togelius, J. (2017). *EvoCommander*: A novel game based on evolving and switching between artificial brains. *IEEE Transactions on Computational Intelligence and AI in Games*, 9(2), 181–191.

Karakovskiy, S., & Togelius, J. (2012). The Mario AI benchmark and competitions. *IEEE Transactions on Computational Intelligence and AI in Games*, 4(1), 55–67.

Koster, R. (2005). *A theory of fun for game designers*. Scottsdale, AZ: Paraglyph Press.

Lantz, F., Isaksen, A., Jaffe, A., Nealen, A., & Togelius, J. (2017). *Depth in strategic games*. Paper presented at the AAAI Workshop on What's Next for AI in Games, San Francisco, CA, February 4. http://movingai.com/aigames17/slides/depth.pdf

Legg, S., & Hutter, M. (2007). Universal intelligence: A definition of machine intelligence. *Minds and Machines*, 17(4), 391–444.

Liapis, A., Yannakakis, G. N., & Togelius, J. (2013). Sentient Sketchbook: Computer-aided game level authoring. In *Proceedings of the Eighth*

International Conference on the Foundations of Digital Games (pp. 213–220). Santa Cruz, CA: Society for the Advancement of the Science of Digital Games.

Loiacono, D., Lanzi, P. L., Togelius, J., Onieva, E., Pelta, D. A., Butz, M. V., ... , Quadflieg, J. (2010). The 2009 Simulated Car Racing Championship. *IEEE Transactions on Computational Intelligence and AI in Games*, 2(2), 131–147.

Machado, T., Nealen, A., & Togelius, J. (2017). CICERO: Computationally Intelligent Collaborative EnviROnment for game and level design. Paper presented at ICCC Computational Creativity & Games Workshop, Atlanta, GA, June 19–23. http://computationalcreativity.net/iccc2017/CCGW/CCGW17_paper_1.pdf

Mahlmann, T., Drachen, A., Togelius, J., Canossa, A., & Yannakakis, G. N. (2010). Predicting player behavior in *Tomb Raider: Underworld*. In *Proceedings of the 2010 IEEE Symposium on Computational Intelligence and Games* (pp. 178–185). Piscataway, NJ: IEEE.

Malone, T. (1981). *What makes computer games fun?* Paper presented at the Joint Conference on Easier and More Productive Use of Computer Systems, Ann Arbor, MI, May 20–22.

Millington, I., & Funge, J. (2009). *Artificial intelligence for games*. Boca Raton, FL: CRC Press.

Mnih, V., Kavukcuoglu, K., Silver, D., Rusu, A. A., Veness, J., Bellemare, M. G., ... , Hassabis, D. (2015). Human-level control through deep reinforcement learning. *Nature*, 518(7540), 529–533.

Nielsen, T. S., Barros, G. A., Togelius, J., & Nelson, M. J. (2015). Towards generating arcade game rules with VGDL. In *Proceedings of the 2015 IEEE Conference on Computational Intelligence and Games* (pp. 185–192). Piscataway, NJ: IEEE.

Ontanón, S., Synnaeve, G., Uriarte, A., Richoux, F., Churchill, D., & Preuss, M. (2013). A survey of real-time strategy game AI research and competition in *StarCraft*. *IEEE Transactions on Computational Intelligence and AI in Games*, 5(4), 293–311.

Orkin, J. (2006). *Three states and a plan: The AI of F.E.A.R.* Presentation given at Game Developers Conference 2006, San Jose, CA, March 20–24.

Pedersen, C., Togelius, J., & Yannakakis, G. N. (2010). Modeling player experience for content creation. *IEEE Transactions on Computational Intelligence and AI in Games,* 2(1), 54–67.

Perez-Liebana, D., Samothrakis, S., Togelius, J., Lucas, S. M., & Schaul, T. (2016). General video game AI: Competition, challenges, and opportunities. In *Proceedings of the 30th AAAI Conference on Artificial Intelligence* (pp. 4335–4337). Palo Alto, CA: AAAI.

Perez-Liebana, D., Samothrakis, S., Togelius, J., Schaul, T., Lucas, S. M., Couëtoux, A., ... Thompson, T. (2016). The 2014 General Video Game Playing Competition. *IEEE Transactions on Computational Intelligence and AI in Games,* 8(3), 229–243.

Russell, S., & Norvig, P. (2009). *Artificial intelligence: A modern approach* (3rd ed.). London, UK: Pearson.

Rusu, A. A., Rabinowitz, N. C., Desjardins, G., Soyer, H., Kirkpatrick, J., Kavukcuoglu, K., ... Hadsell, R. (2016). *Progressive neural networks.* https://arxiv.org/abs/1606.04671

Salen, K., & Zimmerman, E. (2004). *Rules of play: Game design fundamentals.* Cambridge, MA: MIT Press.

Samuel, A. L. (1959). Some studies in machine learning using the game of checkers. *IBM Journal of Research and Development,* 3(3), 210–229.

Schaeffer, J., Burch, N., Björnsson, Y., Kishimoto, A., Müller, M., Lake, R., Lu, P., and Sutphen, S. (2007). Checkers is solved. *Science,* 317(5844), 1518–1522.

Schmidhuber, J. (2006). Developmental robotics, optimal artificial curiosity, creativity, music, and the fine arts. *Connection Science,* 18(2), 173–187.

Shaker, N., Shaker, M., & Togelius, J. (2013). Evolving playable content for cut the rope through a simulation-based approach. In G. Sukthankar & I. Horswill (Eds.), *Proceedings of the 9th AAAI Conference on Artificial*

Intelligence and Interactive Digital Entertainment (pp. 72–78). Palo Alto, CA: AAAI.

Shaker, N., Togelius, J., & Nelson, M. J. (2016). *Procedural content generation in games*. Cham, Switzerland: Springer.

Shaker, N., Yannakakis, G. N., & Togelius, J. (2010). Towards automatic personalized content generation for platform games. In G. M. Youngblood & V. Bulitko (Eds.), *Proceedings of the 6th AAAI Conference on Artificial Intelligence and Interactive Digital Entertainment* (pp. 63–68). Palo Alto, CA: AAAI

Silver, D., Huang, A., Maddison, C. J., Guez, A., Sifre, L., Van Den Driessche, G., … , Hassabis, D. (2016). Mastering the game of Go with deep neural networks and tree search. *Nature*, 529(7587), 484–489.

Silver, D., Hubert, T., Schrittwieser, J., Antonoglou, I., Lai, M., Guez, A., … , Hassabis, D. (2017). *Mastering chess and Shogi by self-play with a general reinforcement learning algorithm*. https://arxiv.org/abs/1712.01815

Smith, A. M., & Mateas, M. (2010). Variations forever: Flexibly generating rulesets from a sculptable design space of mini-games. In *Proceedings of the 2010 IEEE Symposium on Computational Intelligence and Games* (pp. 273–280). Piscataway, NJ: IEEE.

Smith, A. M., & Mateas, M. (2011). Answer set programming for procedural content generation: A design space approach. *IEEE Transactions on Computational Intelligence and AI in Games*, 3(3), 187–200.

Smith, G., Whitehead, J., & Mateas, M. (2011). Tanagra: Reactive planning and constraint solving for mixed-initiative level design. *IEEE Transactions on Computational Intelligence and AI in Games*, 3(3), 201–215.

Stanley, K. O., Bryant, B. D., & Miikkulainen, R. (2005). Real-time neuroevolution in the NERO video game. *IEEE Transactions on Evolutionary Computation*, 9(6), 653–668.

Sweetser, P., & Wyeth, P. (2005). GameFlow: A model for evaluating player enjoyment in games. *Computers in Entertainment*, 3(3). doi:10.1145/1077246.1077253

Tekofsky, S., Van Den Herik, J., Spronck, P., & Plaat, A. (2013). *Psyops: Personality assessment through gaming behavior.* Paper presented at the Eighth International Conference on the Foundations of Digital Games, Chania, Crete, Greece, May 14–17.

Tekofsky, S., Spronck, P., Goudbeek, M., Plaat, A., & van den Herik, J. (2015). Past our prime: A study of age and play style development in *Battlefield 3. IEEE Transactions on Computational Intelligence and AI in Games*, 7(3), 292–303.

Togelius, J., De Nardi, R., & Lucas, S. M. (2007). Towards automatic personalised content creation for racing games. In *Proceedings of the 2007 IEEE Symposium on Computational Intelligence and Games* (pp. 252–259). Piscataway, NJ: IEEE.

Togelius, J., Lucas, S., Thang, H. D., Garibaldi, J. M., Nakashima, T., Tan, C. H., ... , Burrow, P. (2008). The 2007 IEEE CEC simulated car racing competition. *Genetic Programming and Evolvable Machines*, 9(4), 295–329.

Togelius, J., Preuss, M., Beume, N., Wessing, S., Hagelbäck, J., Yannakakis, G. N., Grappiolo, P. (2013). Controllable procedural map generation via multiobjective evolution. *Genetic Programming and Evolvable Machines*, 14(2), 245–277.

Togelius, J., & Schmidhuber, J. (2008). An experiment in automatic game design. In *Proceedings of the 2008 IEEE Symposium On Computational Intelligence and Games* (pp. 111–118). Piscataway, NJ: IEEE.

Togelius, J., Yannakakis, G. N., Stanley, K. O., & Browne, C. (2011). Search-based procedural content generation: A taxonomy and survey. *IEEE Transactions on Computational Intelligence and AI in Games*, 3(3), 172–186.

Treanor, M., Zook, A., Eladhari, M. P., Togelius, J., Smith, G., Cook, M., ... , Smith, A. (2015). *AI-based game design patterns.* Paper presented at the Tenth International Conference on the Foundations of Digital Games, Pacific Grove, CA, June 22–25. http://www.fdg2015.org/papers/fdg2015_paper_23.pdf

Turing, A. M. (1950). Computing machinery and intelligence. *Mind*, 49, 433–460.

Turing, A. M., Bates, M., Bowden, B., and Strachey, C. (1953). Digital computers applied to games. In B. V. Bowden (Ed.), *Faster than thought: Symposium on digital computing machines* (pp. 286–310). London, UK: Pitman.

Vygotsky, L. (1978). Interaction between learning and development. In M. Gauvain & M. Cole (Eds.), *Readings on the development of children* (pp. 34–40). New York, NY: Scientific American Books.

Yannakakis, G. N., & Togelius, J. (2011). Experience-driven procedural content generation. *IEEE Transactions on Affective Computing*, 2(3), 147–161.

Yannakakis, G. N., & Togelius, J. (2018). *Artificial intelligence and games*. Cham, Switzerland: Springer. http://gameaibook.org

Yee, N., Ducheneaut, N., Nelson, L., & Likarish, P. (2011). Introverted elves and conscientious gnomes: The expression of personality in *World of Warcraft* . In *Proceedings of the SIGCHI Conference on Human Factors in Computing Systems* (pp. 753–762). New York, NY: ACM.

Index

Page numbers in italics indicate references to figures.